S.E.A.L.

Sex, Entertainment & Lies

LONDELL "NIKKO LONDON" SMITH
AS TOLD TO **MYA KAY**

THE TMG FIRM

New York

The TMG Firm, LLC
112 W. 34th Street
17th and 18th Floors
New York, NY 10120
www.thetmgfirm.com

S.E.A.L.: Sex, Entertainment & Lies
Copyright © 2016 Londell Smith
Copyright © 2016 Mya K. Douglas
Published by The TMG Firm, LLC

All rights reserved. No part of this book may be reproduced in any form by any means without the prior written consent of the Publisher. For information address The TMG Firm, 112 W. 34th Street,
17th and 18th Floors,
New York, NY 10120.

For more information about special discounts for bulk purchase, please contact The TMG Firm at 1-888-984-3864 ext 12 or publishing@thetmgfirm.com

ISBN: 978-0-99835-652-5
Library of Congress Control Number: 2016963016
All rights reserved

First The TMG Firm Trade Paperback Edition April 2017
Printed in the United States of America

This is a work of creative nonfiction. The events are portrayed to the best of Londell Smith's memory. The conversations in this book all come from the author's recollections, though they are not written to represent word-for-word transcripts. Rather, the author has retold them in a way that evokes the feeling and meaning what was said and in all instances, the essence of the dialogue is accurate. While all the stories in this book are true, some names and identifying details have been changed to protect the privacy of the people involved.

Cover Photo Copyright © 2016 Sean James for Sean James Photography
Cover created and designed by Brittani Williams for
TSPub Creative, LLC.

FOREWORD

The first time I met Nikko; he probably doesn't even remember. First of all, Nikko and I are from the same neck of the woods. He's from Brooklyn, and I lived in every borough except Staten Island. One thing that he and I have in common is that fire that comes out when we have to protect our family and loved ones. That's a part of him that wasn't shown on television.

One day, I was going to eat at Justin's in Manhattan. Nikko was coming out, and he had a gun in his hand. I have no idea what happened inside Justin's, but someone must have pissed him off. I guess seeing me calmed him down. Whatever confrontation he had inside of Justin's caused us to be refused back inside. I decided to do the brotherly thing and lent my support. Here it was, I didn't know him, but I saw another brother in a bad spot.

We started talking, just shooting the breeze until he calmed down. Once he got into the car, I felt like *okay cool, he's good.* One thing I've learned is that you don't want to see that side of Nikko. We try our best to protect our families and our people, so if that unleashes the dragon, so be it. That's something I appreciate about him. He's humble, but he's cocky when necessary. More often than not, you will see the humble person with unlimited talent who aches to make music.

I've seen many opportunities that he's taken. I'm still stuck and trying to figure out why this guy isn't in the music business full time. His talent is unheard of, but people just didn't understand him. When I first started, people didn't understand what I was doing either.

I see the people he looked out for, people he was loyal to and who just didn't give him his just due. With his artistry and his success, I've seen many opportunities that Nikko has taken and it seems to me like the promises made to him were never kept. He would get the record deal, but then things would fall through, and Nikko wouldn't get his fair share.

If you're living in New York and you have talent, there are opportunities for you to make something of yourself. But there's still no guarantee that you're going to make it all the way. To me, his talent should've been out there. Most times when you have someone like Nikko who brings so much to the table, there's going to be people who feel intimidated.

That's the reason why I primarily played the background. Nikko's audience is all females. They love this cat. This is a guy that people knew even before he had a record deal. Nikko was famous before he was famous if that makes sense. He could walk into a spot, and people saw a star. His talent is better than his look, and he's definitely marketable. I feel the promises made to him in the music business weren't kept because they felt he would become better than them. They felt he would surpass them.

I would love to see Nikko do his thing. I always put out every artist I signed. To see someone signing people just to hold them back is crazy, but it happens. You have individuals who don't want you to become larger than them. I've seen people sign artists to fail them and I'm just not with that.

To me, this book is part of Nikko's catalog of success. He's also a well-known fitness strategist, not just an instructor. I've seen him work with people where he's educating them and walking them through what's best for their needs. One thing I want people to get from this is to know that no one got him to where he is now. He got himself here, and he's always been well connected. I know this book will be successful and people will see him in a different light. It's just one moment of many moments that he has to continue to shine. Only this time, no one can dim his light.

–Teddy Riley
Grammy Award Winning Singer-Songwriter and Record Producer

"Sometimes people think they know you. They know a few facts about you, and they piece you together in a way that makes sense to them. And if you don't know yourself very well, you might even believe that they are right. But the truth is, that isn't you. That isn't you at all."

–Leila Sales

INTRODUCTION
The Man, The Myth, The Story

There is a truth I want you to know. I've stayed quiet for so long because I realize often people find it less complicated to buy into the available false reality than to dig deeper for the truth. This is not an attempt to defame anyone or devalue the opportunity that placed me in the position to tell you this story. It's to regain what was essentially taken away from me - my humanity. This is the no fluff, authentic moment of Nikko London. The face of the most hated man on reality television. What most people fail to realize is I was Nikko before *Love & Hip Hop: Atlanta*. Nikko London has walked with legends and had successful moments in the entertainment business long before the nemesis of reality television came to life.

I was a strong force in music, a valuable asset to the community and always a hustler with a strong entrepreneurial spirit. The place where we met is just a moment in my life; it's not *the* moment of my life. My goal is to help you see beyond the camera lens to who I am before, during and after *Love & Hip Hop: Atlanta*. Without this story, the truth would not be accurate. The relationship I had on the show is only a few years of the several decades I've been on this earth.

I am not upset that you define me according to what you think you know. I understand that 'perception is reality,' so this leads you to conclude you know a person. However, I believe in the adage "Believe none of what you hear and only half of what you see." This is one of those moments where that saying rings true louder than ever. Most of what you see on television is fabricated, even on so-called 'reality television.' Entertainment is interesting in many ways because it allows you to participate in a conversation with people who have shared interests.

The challenge of being on reality television is it's a one-way conversation. The only feedback from the audience comes in the number of television viewers; not questions and comments to which you can respond in real time. Being as such, there are limited chances to address questions, concerns or even well wishes. This results in the dehumanizing of reality stars. Social media helps, but viewers' questions are often lost in a sea of trolls searching for the next person to turn into a meme. The reunion shows are not the appropriate platform to have our voices heard. They tend to rehash the drama and mistakes of the past season, thereby only solidifying viewer's previous estimates of you. Further complicating matters is the brevity of focus on individual cast members and bias in favor of the network's interests. The truth is, regardless of what really occurred in any given situation or who you actually are; the show will continue to create a story line that revolves around the narrative they are willing to perpetuate.

So this is my conversation - this is my story and my answers to all of the questions and statements that were thrown at me via blogs and social media. Most people didn't even ask me any questions. They assumed and told their story based on a few facts. Now, this is my chance to clear the air. This is my chance to speak about Londell "Nikko London" Smith. As a black man, there's always going to be a myth circulating about me - whether it's the media tearing me down because of my television story, America tearing me down because of the color of my skin or the stereotypes that surround my race. There's always going to be something.

In your hands are my truths – my narrative that will be around just as long as the rumors and lies. Even longer than *Love & Hip Hop: Atlanta* airs and the blogs continue with their bogus stories. They say once it's out there, it's out there, so I'm pleased to put my story out there. I'm elated you get to meet the guy who was raised in Brooklyn, New York, Flatbush to be precise. The one who always found a way to live and thrive on his gifts and passion for life. The guy who can make a dollar out of fifteen cents and who never completely lost sight of his purpose. I may have become lost for a minute, as we all do, but being lost helped me find myself again. You do something on the scale of *Love & Hip Hop: Atlanta* and you discover more than you know. You find out how to make an opportunity work for you.

I want to be clear; my story is not meant to shape anyone else's truth. It's simply to speak my own, so the world knows Nikko's humanity is bigger than a moment on reality television. It's larger than all the mistakes I made as a kid growing up in Brooklyn. It's even more important than a steamy relationship or love triangle. I want you not only to see me but all reality stars as people who have stories to tell. Stories that are tainted on television and stories that are built to make the cast member look less favorable. At any given moment, I don't have a problem letting you know who I am, what I do and who I love. This again is that moment. Prayerfully, by the time you're done, I'll progress from being the most hated man on reality television to the 'most respected man on reality television.' There's no need for everyone to love me. That would be fake, but by the end of this book; you will respect me. That, I can guarantee.

SEX

CHAPTER 1
Where It All Began

I met Wendy Jefferson in New York back in 1997. We had mutual friends that were in the same circle. Wendy, who later became Mimi's manager, was instantly attracted to me as I was to her. I was in a relationship at the time, but my girlfriend and I were having serious issues. For me, meeting Wendy had perfect timing. She was pursuing acting, and I was still pursuing my music. We started hanging out with each other and began sleeping together about twice a week. Every time we reconnected, even if we lost communication, it would result in us having sex. We had mutual respect for each other, and no one knew about our sexual escapades. To my surprise, I saw her years later at an event in L.A. standing with Mimi, who I already knew from the music industry scene. Then, the next night I saw them together, I learned *Love & Hip Hop: Atlanta* would be in my future.

I was living in L.A., hustling and pursuing my music. The scene during that time was much different. I was making moves in music and working with people like the late great Gerald Levert and Tamia. Let the world tell it,

NIKKO LONDON

Love & Hip Hop: Atlanta gave me my talent, but that's not how it all started. Before running into Mimi and getting the opportunity to work on *Love & Hip Hop: Atlanta*, I was working with a pop group. They were talented, and in my opinion, they were the next One Direction. I was always an investor, and this situation wasn't any different. I believed in all they embodied, and I wanted to help secure a music deal. The deal I was working on was with recording artist Akon and executive Johnny Wright, who managed Justin Timberlake and other amazing artists.

All was going well when suddenly, things took a turn for the worse. Once parents and lawyers began to bump heads, the situation automatically shifted in the wrong direction. That's one of the challenging obstacles when working with children in the music business. People such as myself know the business, and the parents know their children, but assume they know the business. This was when the dynamics began to shift. The deal wasn't going very well because, in the ninth inning, the confusion between the parents ruined everything.

Once the parents pulled out, it made it challenging for me to continue working with the group. Here it was, the opportunity of a lifetime for these young guys, but egos and opinions blocked their blessing. The music business is hard enough with just a few people involved, so when you add indecisive parents, it can become a disaster. This would have been my opportunity to be in the game on a huge level and secure another moment in music. Up to this point, I had already experienced several successful moments. Once again, my career in music wasn't going as I planned. Still, I was building the connections I needed and was receiving attention from major labels. When the deal with the group went array, it felt like I was at ground zero all over again.

Ironically, my journey in entertainment and music spans over twenty years. I've been signed to Sony Records, EMI Records, and Virgin Records. Most people aren't aware of this because reality television only provides you with fifteen minutes of fame. It's not always the appropriate amount of time you need to make yourself shine. You can shine, but the show isn't going to permit you to do it in a positive light. When people saw me on *Love & Hip Hop: Atlanta*, they perceived me to be a leech who used Mimi to further my career. In reality, I was a powerhouse by myself, long before I met her.

I was an artist with EMI Records, during the same time recording artist D'Angelo was signed to the label. I was also signed to Virgin Records around the time recording artist Tank was on their roster. The label executives were so impressed with my talents; they had the late great recording artist Gerald Levert, compose a song for me called "Why Do Girls Love Harder." The fact that I was able to perform a song written by him shows my true singing capabilities. Doors were opening again, and at that time I believed this was finally my moment. It turned out I was wrong; the music industry is a fickle business. Even if you have the goods, the looks and the fan base, when a change occurs at the top, it happens to everyone. People often think because an artist is no longer with a label or things didn't work out, it's because the artist wasn't talented enough. That's far from the truth. A perfect example is what happened with Philadelphia rap group State Property. Those guys are super talented, but when the partnership between Roc-A-Fella Records and Def Jam Records became disrupted, things changed. That's just the way it is.

In my case, a similar situation happened. EMI Records was later sold, and it became a publishing company, which it remains today. Although my first single on EMI Records was composed by the late great Gerald Levert, unfortunately, it was recorded during the change of the corporate structure. Thankfully, I was fortunate enough to be released from my contract without having to pay back any funds from my advance. Later on, I was offered a deal with Virgin Records, which was the most lucrative deal I could secure at the time. I had just returned from an extended hiatus from music, and Virgin Records was performing pretty well as a record label. During this period, I began working with Barry Hankerson, the uncle of the late great recording artist Aaliyah. Our relationship was exclusively based on their relationship with her. After she sadly passed away, the label and Barry couldn't find common ground for all of us to remain in business together. Once again, I was out on a limb and wondering the destination of my music career.

Each time I had a label deal, it fell through. It was like I had bad luck in the music business. Imagine being with some of the best labels in the business, being in a great position and not being able to complete one album. I was so frustrated with what I was experiencing. I had composed songs for artists, such as Case, Tamia and ran with heavy weights, such as Teddy Riley and LL Cool J. Even with all of that success, I couldn't obtain the break I needed. Without the support of a label, I ended up once again searching for my next moment in music. My next moment eventually arrived, but it wasn't in the form of a music opportunity. It was in the form of television.

If you consider the fact that *Love & Hip Hop* is supposed to be based on artists, one would conclude it was another opportunity in music. Somehow I knew this time would be different.

It was the weekend of the 2012 VMA's, which was before the airing of the second season of *Love & Hip Hop: Atlanta*. The weekend was filled with back to back events, and everyone who was anyone was in L.A. As fate would have it, Mimi, her manager Wendy and I were coincidentally at the same party in the JW Marriott. At some point in the night, Wendy and her two companions noticed me through the crowd. Before long, we were deeply engaged in conversation updating each other on our various upcoming projects. All in all the night was a good one. I celebrated the VMA's to the fullest, and as the night progressed, I sporadically interacted with both Mimi and Wendy. I thought nothing special of our encounters, especially since I had known Mimi for years. As they say, hindsight is twenty-twenty, even when it's only looking hours into the past. Looking back at the moment when Wendy first walked over, I realized her companions weren't just her friends; they were key players at VH1. By the end of the party, after speaking with Mimi and Wendy, I had a strong feeling the producers of *Love & Hip Hop: Atlanta* were interested in me. I would soon find out my assumption was correct.

Since the airing of the show, there's been a common misconception that I approached *Love & Hip Hop: Atlanta* or that I used Mimi for the exposure. Both notions are incorrect. I had already known Mimi since 1998. We had about thirteen years of cordial history before the first season of *Love & Hip Hop: Atlanta* aired. Most importantly, VH1 approached me; not the other way around.

A few days after the party, I sat at dinner and listened to how I would be a great love interest for Mimi on the second season of the show. The producers made the proposal interesting, and I couldn't shake the great feeling that a lot of good could come from being on a hit reality show. For one, I had a genuine interest in Mimi long before the possibility of being on the show. If I was on the show, I could use the time to get to know her even better. Even in this simple plan, there was one small hiccup. Wendy and I had been sexually intimate numerous times. Understandably so, Wendy advised me not to mention this to anyone, not even to Mimi. I kept that secret until this very moment. Mimi had no idea her future television boyfriend had been sexually involved with her manager.

Although I was being pursued, that night I left dinner with a few questions. Would the producers do more than express an interest and was I willing to open myself to the world of reality television? I mulled over the idea, and after speaking with one of my good friends, I realized this was the perfect opportunity to break back into the music business successfully.

When I returned to Brooklyn, I spoke with my mother and my family about the possibility of being on reality television. They all thought it would be a great idea. My mother's blessing gave me the feeling something special was about to happen. I had my family's support, and they shared my idea it could help my music career since it wasn't going as well as we all hoped. Of course, instead of this story being told it's painted as if I was a desperate fiend who needed a big Hollywood break. How could that be if I'd been signed to major labels and worked with legends? I wasn't even watching *Love & Hip Hop: Atlanta* at the time. I didn't live in a cave, so I knew about the show, but I wasn't watching reality television when they approached me. Naïve to the depths of reality television, I decided to take a chance and dove in head-first. A few days passed, and I hadn't heard back from Wendy or the producers. I was now heavily interested, but I didn't receive the call confirming my placement on the show.

NIKKO LONDON

While I waited for the update, I continued my usual life in New York. The day before the show was set to air; I received a call from Wendy letting me know Mimi was scheduled to be in D.C. It didn't take long to realize I could use this time to build a relationship with her. I knew spending time with her in D.C. would be enough to establish a connection. Being as this would be my first time dealing with reality television, I was unsure of the behind the scenes process. I figured if they were asking me to be her love interest, at the bare minimum we needed to make it appear real. That night after a fashion show I attended was over, I went straight to the airport and flew to D.C.

When I arrived in D.C., a car service courtesy of the show awaited my arrival. The car waiting for me was a clear indication there was still an active interest. Then ensued the immediate buzz from the blogs. The rumors were circulating that Mimi had a new significant other. People began speculating the identity of the guy, and that sparked her interest. Her relationship with Stevie J. was highly publicized, and it was evident they weren't happy. The hype surrounding Mimi's mystery man swirled while I was in D.C. and continued as I returned to New York. Later in the week, Mimi called and personally asked me to be her love interest on the show.

In the midst of being booked for the show and filming, I had an epiphany of what my actual purpose was. I was the missing ingredient they needed to shape Mimi's storyline entirely; I was the necessary evil. Without our

SEX, ENTERTAINMENT & LIES

relationship and the drama that would develop from it, her storyline wasn't very relevant. All of the significant similarities were there. Stevie and I both were from New York and came from musical backgrounds. It was like applying the finishing touches to an elegant piece of furniture. Once this fact was solidified in my mind, I was convinced me and my music had a chance. That night, I packed everything and drove fourteen hours down to Atlanta. The entire ride, I kept thinking about how great of an opportunity this was to get my name back out there, introduce my music to the world and work in television. It was like killing three birds with one stone.

Once I arrived in Atlanta the scene was nothing like I had imagined. Where I first envisioned possibilities, I now saw a scene that reminded me of David and Goliath. I was David, the kid with stones ready to conquer the world, but VH1 was Goliath. They were big, they were strong and not afraid to abuse their power. The only difference with my story was I wasn't confident the underdog would win this time. I lived in Atlanta for two months, financing everything myself without any contact from the show - no calls from producers, nothing. By now, Mimi and I were dating seriously, and we were connecting in a big way. I enjoyed spending time with her off camera. However, I couldn't help but inquire about the filming for the show. I'm sure I got on her nerves with my constant questioning, especially since she didn't have any answers. I just couldn't help myself. Here I am, living in Atlanta, money dwindling and just waiting around. I'd moved my entire life to be with her and appear on the show. It sounds a little opportunistic, but it was far from it. At least in the way, most people would think. I wasn't using Mimi, but I had plans for the show. The fact is; I didn't want to fail again. In the past, my other projects didn't pan out as expected and I couldn't let that happen again.

In addition to the waiting, I had to deal with being a grown ass man sneaking around like I was in grade school. Although Mimi and Stevie were going through a tumultuous time, she still loved him. While I didn't expect her to get over him in twenty-four hours, I wasn't receptive to the sneaking and hiding. The only reason I initially accepted it was to protect her. Anytime we were out; she was fearful someone would see us and make her life with Stevie ten times worse. As time passed, it became increasingly difficult to go along with it; all while still not filming. I soon began to run out of money and patience. I was getting annoyed facing the fact I'd moved to Atlanta to be on the show, yet the show wasn't delivering their part.

The producers were moving at their pace without the slightest consideration for me, and I wasn't pleased. I signed on with the idea we would be filming and heading in a forward direction. Here I was waiting, while they were slowly dragging along and putting me in an awkward position with Mimi. I began to rethink my decision and felt I made a mistake. I didn't blame Mimi, but I was honestly confused as to why she didn't know more about the status of the show. She had asked me to be a part of this, and I felt she should've been able to let me know what was happening behind the scene. All she kept doing was directing me to the main producer of the show who never called with an explanation. During my waiting period, Mimi and Stevie hit a rough patch. That catapulted her into an incredibly emotional space. My advice to her was simple; *fight back!*

From what I could gather, Stevie and the show felt they had the upper hand because Mimi just wasn't defending herself. I didn't like that at all. I wanted her to realize the position she held, so I encouraged her to be strong. With my support, I helped her gain enough strength to address everything that was wrongfully being stated. I knew without confronting the issue; matters would only continue to worsen. My point to her was: if the show needs your story, then you need to make them realize your worth. By allowing them to take full advantage of her wasn't serving any purpose and only caused her to doubt herself. That prompted her to do the radio interview with Egypt on V-103 The People's Station.

That interview was the catalyst we both needed to open the door. Before going on air, I told Mimi the only way to make an impact was to work together and put our relationship out in the open. At that point, we had nothing to lose, and there wasn't any risk in trying it my way. When it was time for the interview with Egypt, I told her we should do the interview together. It was time to come out of the shadows. I was fed up with hiding the truth. That day, Mimi introduced me as her new boyfriend, and I supported her by publicly stating she was the one for me. Our chemistry was magnetic throughout the entire interview. It was so intense; Egypt and her team acknowledged it immediately. They contacted Stevie to call the station, but he refused. Once the interview aired, our goal was accomplished. Everyone was talking about it, and the show couldn't continue to ignore me. It only made sense. How could they deny me after Mimi announced on the radio she'd moved on from their star player, Stevie? I'm not certain about their consensus at the time; however, I finally got the official call from the show. We had forced the producer's hand.

The aftermath of the interview was great, and we gained a lot of momentum. Shortly thereafter, I was disappointed because it didn't deliver all that I expected. Considering the phone call came directly after the interview, I believed the producers recognized the real connection between us. Even though our storyline was genuine, the ultimate decision of how it would unfold was at the mercy of the producers. The disheartening part of it all is that I wasn't even paid for that season. It sounds outrageous, but I agreed because I was in a desperate situation. I viewed it all as exposure and the most logical route to get my name back in the game. I focused on two facts: I didn't have to audition, and I could capitalize off what initially attracted the producers. So, even though I wasn't being paid millions of dollars or any dollars for that matter, there were other ways to monetize my appearance on the show. There would be club appearances and hosting events; both of which would afford me income and more exposure. I'm not ashamed to admit *Love & Hip Hop: Atlanta* came into my life at a time where I was lower than I would have liked, but the show in no way birthed Nikko London.

Titling this chapter "Where It All Started" is not to give the impression my connection to the show is what made me 'someone.' This is not what the title means at all. The title marks a period in my life where it was opened for the world to view; only I wasn't permitted to show my complete life. As it turned out, the amount of time I filmed wasn't aligned with the time aired in the final edits. Instead of getting to know me, audiences saw mere glimpses, given in intervals of minutes of who I truly am. Herein lies the importance of this book. It has provided me the freedom and space to tell my story the way it actually happened, without edits or cutaways. It allows people to get to know the real Londell "Nikko London" Smith.

It's always been said you never get a second chance to make a first impression. I hope like hell this isn't true! All of my initial plans of introducing Nikko the artist failed miserably. The name Nikko was out there, but it was attached to someone I didn't embody. Am I willing to say everything about me was false? No, but the image was incomplete. My character was judged by a half second of realism and a half second of forced interaction used to create an entertaining reality. To be clear, I'm not bitter, and I will never hate the game or the players in it. I'm just ready to play the game my way!

CHAPTER 2
Marrying Margeaux

The first thing I noticed was her stunning beauty. She was exotic, and it made me stop in my tracks. Her looks captured me, as her beauty and body moved me. The feeling I had at first sight of her told me something good was going to happen between the two of us. We walked up to the club at the very same time. She walked towards the line with a few friends. I had a reserved table and knew I was heading straight to the front of the line. As soon as I saw her, I grabbed her hand and said to her "you're with me." Yes, it was a bold move. That's always been my style, and she was attracted to that quality. From that moment on, I knew she was the Bonnie to my Clyde. After that first night, I could tell she was the one I could be with for the rest of share my life. As cliché as it sounds, it's not some Romeo bs; it's the truth.

Margeaux came into my life at the perfect time. When I met her, I was leaving a nine-year relationship, and my ex and I weren't in a good space at the time. I soon learned she was heavy into fashion and had an interest in music. Although I knew her interests, I had no idea together we would create magic. From my perspective, she was always "the one." Early on, we spent time together every night discovering how much we had in common. Since *Love & Hip Hop: Atlanta* has aired I've been painted as a male whore, but I'm more of a long-term relationship type of guy. As I've said before, I was with my ex before Margeaux for nine years, and I've been with Margeaux for ten years. I may not have been perfect in my relationships, but I've always had great intentions with all of the women I have dated.

Margeaux and I married quickly, but I felt good about the decision. I would have married her under any circumstances, but she was a Canadian resident that needed a green card. Normally, this would not have been a problem, but an investor we were working with threatened to have her deported because he and I had a major disagreement. I couldn't and wasn't going to let that happen. She and I were totally into each other. The love was growing between the two of us, and we were taking care of business. It all felt right. We were making great business connections and recording her album. We did a song called "Super Fly"; it was a hit. There was something about the way our music fused together that made me realize we had something powerful. Often times, the music became bigger than the marriage and it wasn't always easy. I learned the hard way that if you're going to work with your significant other, you have to keep your business and personal separate. The business can't impact the marriage, and the marriage can't affect the business. When it does, it can hurt it a great deal.

For a marriage or business arrangement to work, it needs to be built on a solid foundation. I was trying to build both at the same time. It was like walking on a tight-rope. If I put too much into one, the other could easily fail. What would I have gained if the business aspect of our relationship succeeded and the marriage failed or vice versa? When I entered the relationship, I wasn't sure how things would work out, but I had faith it would be okay. How could it result in any other way? We had many common interests and clicked on so many different levels. There was always the chance something could have gone wrong or situations could have become strained. Honestly, I never thought that it would happen, but it did. More than likely, emotionally it attributed to Margeaux and I going in different directions.

When we became an item, I had no idea she was into women. In fact, I didn't find out until later in our relationship after things were beginning to fall apart. Our union was full of patterns and tension. We were simply going through the motions and to the point where avoiding separation seemed impossible. While this whirlwind was occurring, she expressed she was feeling restricted. Margeaux felt she was born for more and stressed the possibility of being with a woman. I listened carefully to all she shared and heard everything; even the things she did not say. I began to understand why she felt like I was holding her back.

Although our marriage wasn't at its strongest point, we always had a close friendship, and I wanted her to be happy. I told her to explore her feelings for women. If that's what she needed to be free, then I didn't want to be the one to prevent that from happening. Besides, by that point, our marriage didn't matter much because we were only coexisting to pacify each other. It may sound strange, but Margeaux's interest in women was a softer blow to me than if she would've said she was interested in another man. Sure, I questioned it, and I was curious as to what this meant for us, but I figured this would show her I cared more about what she desired.

It was at this time, while my marriage was in transition that I became involved with *Love & Hip Hop: Atlanta*. When I initially asked Margeaux to come on the show, she said "no." She said, "I don't want any parts of the ratchet, ghetto-mess." It just didn't seem to fit her personality because she wasn't into drama. From what she knew about the show, *Love & Hip Hop: Atlanta* was just that; drama. So, naturally, she was against the idea of appearing on the show. As time passed, she began to hear more about herself and our marriage in the blogs as well as around town. This is when she finally decided she didn't have any choice other than to defend herself. One of the worst rumors that bothered her was that she and I set-up Mimi; since it pertained to the sex tape especially. She knew that was furthest from the truth. Even with my wife's disdain for the show, our friendship took a front seat once again. Margeaux wasn't going to allow me to be lied on and victimized. She knew Mimi wasn't a victim and felt everyone else should be aware. Although, initially she was very upset when she learned about the sex tape.

    I distinctly remember the day I told her about the sex tape. It was a month before it was set to be released. I was still living in Atlanta, and she was residing in New York. I didn't think it would be fair for her to find out at the same time as the public. I called, told her everything and the news hit her hard. She immediately started crying and questioned how I could do something so damaging to our friendship. Yes, we were separated, but she still wondered how I could betray her with another woman in public. I defended myself by pointing out that she was seeing other people as well. She responded by insinuating I did the sex tape as revenge and accusing me of not loving her. I was fed up with hearing her make these false accusations. My mistakes and even my shortcomings didn't equate to me not loving Margeaux. After all was said and done, she came through like the rider she is - she had my back. She would not sit idly by and let the show perpetuate the fallacy I played Mimi, and she was unaware of the sex tape. Margeaux wanted to make it clear I wasn't playing anyone, not even her. Although she had initially turned down the offer to appear on the show, she later agreed now was the time to make her debut appearance.

    Margeaux and I aren't perfect people, but we are transparent with each other without lies and deceit. We felt the only way the sex tape and rumors surrounding it would be diminished was by her explaining her side of the story. Margeaux and I weren't together from the onset of my relationship with MiMi. We were separated for years, and that's exactly what she said on national television. I didn't force her to say anything against her will. How could I? Besides, Mimi was well aware of my relationship with Margeaux. She knew our relationship ended. However, she didn't know I was legally married. I didn't set out to keep my marital status from her for underhanded reasons. I just didn't feel our relationship was at the point where I could divulge that information. More importantly, I wasn't going to jeopardize Margeaux's life in the United States for a television show.

After being married, my perspective on marriage is filled with mixed emotions. Now that I look at my marriage, and I see we had an all for one mentality. Throughout it all, I did what I had to do to make sure we survived, even if it meant our marriage might suffer. While growing up, I saw my father who was married to my mother, leaving our home to visit my sisters and brothers birthed from his adulterous ways. He had four children with his wife, my mother, but he also had three outside children. This opened my eyes to the different ways our families were treated. I saw my father put his family first. I watched him make the right decisions, but I also watched him make the wrong decisions. By the time my mother remarried, I was in my early twenties and moved out on my own.

Suffice it to say, while growing up I didn't have a strong example of marriage. I learned how a man takes financial care of his family, but the emotional model was nonexistent. Nonetheless, my father showed me the image of a family. I saw my family saying grace before dinner, having family time together and making sure we were academically performing well. It was like we were the picture perfect family, except being married didn't prevent my father from seeing other women. Witnessing this conflicting account of marriage shaped my views on what it entailed. I learned from the inside it can appear like it's all going well, but there can be infidelity amongst other things. I also discovered a child could be adequately nurtured by their parents, while they fight and argue with each other.

With my skewed concept of family and marriage, I probably wasn't the best candidate for a successful union. My ideology was severely jaded, but with her, I let my guard completely down. It was effortless for me to be vulnerable with someone who was inspirational and compelled me to be no one other than myself. Art and music tied us together, and through it, I wanted to share more of myself, including my life vision.

I cared for Margeaux from the very beginning. The fact that she could see our interdependence was bigger than us only made me care for her more. The hustle and the mission combined made our bond stronger. As we moved along, it becomes more evident we both together and separately had incredible gifts to share with the world. It wasn't just about the industry - it was about purpose. It was a blessing for me to meet a woman like her. Once I let her all the way in; I was with her. I had her back against anything no matter what. From that point, it was always us.

Margeaux was with me during one of the hardest times of my life; homelessness in Los Angeles. I was living in L.A. before she arrived and in about two months earned approximately $80,000 by managing a producer and doing some consultant work. With cash in hand, I sent for her to be with me in the City of Angels. This ended up being a bad move on my part because I didn't have a solid plan together before sending for her. We quickly fell deep into our music. While being caught in the rapture of the artistry, we lost sight of the business aspect. To make matters worse, I was spending money and investing in things for Margeaux, all while being the only one with an income. The unbalanced outflow of money put a strain on our finances. It got to the point where there were only a few dollars left and paying rent became a challenge. We ended up moving all of our possessions in storage and began living out of the studio.

While we plotted our next moves, we ate cheap food to keep what little money we had in our pockets. It's not my proudest moment as an adult, but sometimes I had my mother send me a few bucks to keep us above water. My only option was borrowing money from my mother because there wasn't anyone in the business I could ask without a word of my struggles traveling around. Even on the off chance someone was willing to keep my secret, I couldn't risk the exposure, so borrowing money from industry colleagues wasn't a consideration. During this time there was always underlying tension with Margeaux. She was a suburban girl from Canada and wasn't used to any of the uncertainties. Nonetheless, she stayed in the grind with me, which I will always appreciate. She could've easily called home and told her parents to rescue her, but she rode it out with me. There was a light at the end of the tunnel for a brief moment. A project I was working on seemed to be going well, but it didn't pan out as I had hoped.

Although things weren't working out as we had expected, we continued to put forth an effort by exploring new things. Nothing seemed to work on a long-term basis. Soon Margeaux and I were at a point so low we started to feel like there had to better answers out there. One day while driving down Sunset Boulevard we saw the Church of Scientology. At the sight of the large building, we began discussing all of the things we'd heard about the religion and decided we had nothing to lose by finding out the details of the faith. We parked, walked inside and toured the church. Before the tour began, we had to take a test to get a feel for who we were and to determine where we would be placed during our visit. The format of the exam was synonymous to an IQ test.

It felt like we'd walked into another world. Everyone that we passed along the tour was so robotic. They appeared happy, but something about them felt stiff and forced. As the tour ended, Margeaux and I were informed that we had to return to obtain the test results from the test we had taken earlier. As we prepared to leave we were provided with information on the two programs the church offered. The first option offered free room and board with a monthly stipend if we were to join the church. This seemed pretty good until we learned we would be obligated to work for the church for life in exchange. The second option was both less severe and generous. This option afforded us the opportunity to become part of their programs if we purchased the books supplied by the church. Although it sounds a little off-putting, at the time our hope was someone would be able to point us in the right direction spiritually. Our thirst had us open to trying something different. Margeaux and I both shared the thought the Church of Scientology couldn't be that bad if many of the Hollywood's elite were members. It wasn't long before I felt conflicted by what I was hearing and what I was feeling.

Something felt off to me, but I was admittedly drawn into listening as they spoke in soft and soothing tones. As they were selling Margeaux and me on why we should purchase their books, their voices reassured us we needed them. When it was all said and done, I ended up spending about $70 on books. No sooner than we arrived at the car, Margeaux turned to me and said, "you're not reading this book." Both of us sat briefly silent before she asked, "how did they even get us to buy this?" Neither of us had the answer. It felt odd they had us pay for the book to study the programs of their church without them providing or even offering any literature to help understand the basics of their religion. In past experiences and to my knowledge, when you visit a religious organization they typically do their best to help you understand the basics of their beliefs; whether by conversation or some literature. Generally, this happens before you're asked to buy something. The other thing that struck me as odd was their method of coyly coercing you to become a member of their church, almost without you even realizing what was happening. They say all of the right things, in the right way, but you can feel that something isn't right. They were more than willing to take advantage of us being at our most vulnerable position. They sensed we were at our lowest point and was ready to try anything. I found out later, once I was involved with Mimi, I had made the right decision by avoiding that religion.

After we had failed in our efforts to find spiritual guidance, Margeaux and I were back at square one. We returned to our temporary place at the studio and resumed living there where we stayed for six weeks. Two months into being homeless, Margeaux and I decided we had enough, so we packed up all of our belongings and decided to return to New York. Thankfully, we didn't have to finish the lease in the studio space. The landlords were very understanding and let us break the terms of the contract. We immediately left the studio behind, hopped in my truck and headed back to New York. Being as it was the quickest route from California to New York, we decided to drive the northern route. We figured we would save precious time and gas on the long trip. What neither of us knew was we would end up driving directly through a blizzard. In Nebraska, we hit the worst of the storm and was able only to drive about ten miles per hour, adding countless hours to our trip. As an alternative, we considered pulling over and waiting out the storm. We changed our minds once we realized there was a chance the truck would end up covered by the large amounts of falling snow. Slowly but steadily we safely made it through the storm. However, by the time we arrived in Virginia we ran out of gas and even worse, we also ran out of money. Thankfully, my mother pulled through for us and wired money for food and gas. Even with the setbacks and me doing all of the driving, the trip only took us a total of three days.

We arrived in New York and moved in with my mother who was kind enough to let us move in the upstairs apartment of her brownstone. The move wasn't particularly easy on Margeaux. She was stressed about the move from L.A. and not having accomplished many of the goals she had set for herself while we lived there. I did my best to remain positive and continued to encourage her. I wanted more than anything for her to understand that despite everything that had happened we were going to be okay. I didn't have any other choice but to be the strong one since by this point she was pulling from my strength. We lived with my mother for about eight months. The entire time I hustled and did everything I could to get back on my feet.

Times were difficult, and we both did our best to cope. I can be honest and say I probably didn't give Margeaux all the love she needed. I guess I couldn't give her the love she desired. The type of love she saw growing up. Margeaux was raised in a home with both married parents and a stable family structure. Her parents were like the Huxtables. She had sisters she was close with, and her family had a bond I hadn't thoroughly experienced. Unlike my family life growing up, there was no underlying dysfunction in her home. Although I always had her best interest at heart, I was constantly searching for success and always thinking about the business. It was easy for her to believe I only cared about her regarding what we could do together in business. I easily fell into the role of the provider because it was innately within me. I was wired to figure out a way to make money and keep your family fed. I was grinding so hard it slipped my mind that she needed more than financial support; she needed love.

As an artist and someone who's used to making money, I had a drive for business more than I had a need to nurture and reassure someone. Margeaux often voiced her concerns about the way I expressed my love. Better yet, the lack of expression in the way that best suited her emotions and needs. It only made matters worse that we kept our marriage as private as possible; I did it for the sake of her music. I only wanted her to succeed and for all of her musical aspirations to come true. It wasn't necessarily what she wanted, but I showed her love by handling her business and doing my best to make sure she was good. I wanted people to see her talent and artistry; not just as the girlfriend or wife of Nikko. The focus rightfully belonged on the music, not our relationship. In her mind, she took this as me saying I didn't love her.

If I could name one major defining moment in our marriage, it would be when we formed a group called 'Test Drive.' As a group, we had one of our first records produced by record producer Timbaland and vocal producer Jim Beanz. The song was called "Super Fly" and at first, listen we knew we had a hit. In fact, I knew it as soon as I composed it. We filmed the video for the song in the Chinatown section of Manhattan with a simple boombox behind us. Between the song and our energy, we drew a large crowd. So many people gathered around us traffic began to back up – it was crazy, and we loved it.

The vibe between us solidified the thought that together we're unstoppable. If we could create such a moment on a corner in Chinatown, then we could conquer the world musically. When I gazed into the building crowd, I dreamed we were halfway across the world performing in Europe. Unfortunately, like all things, the moment eventually came to an end. Subsequently, we were back to being a married couple who still hadn't found a consistent groove in our relationship. I was just too focused on our careers.

As I've stressed numerous times, my intentions weren't wrong. I wanted to be the man Margeaux expected, but I didn't know how to balance giving 100%

to our career aspirations while still having enough to give to the relationship. To complicate matters further, I never had an actual example of how to properly conduct myself in a committed relationship. I was learning as I went along and quickly began to fall in the statistical percentile of marriages that fail. I'm not blaming my upbringing for my imperfections; however, it places many of my behaviors into perspective.

Around 2006 is when my "business first" approach to our marriage began to take its toll and Margeaux began to push away from our relationship. At the time I was in Miami attempting to make things happen, while she was still in New York. We did our best to hold it together. There were just too many miles between us, and I didn't have the means to get her down to Miami with me. The tension was thick, and during our ups and downs, her father fell gravely ill. Regrettably, she didn't have her green card fully processed so she couldn't leave the U.S. without being denied access upon her return from Canada. Sadly, she never made it to the hospital to say her final goodbye. Thankfully, she was able to attend his funeral service.

After her father's death, things between us grew worse. A conversation between her and her father before his passing had an immediate effect on our already strained relationship. One day Margeaux asked her father, "if a guy doesn't tell you he loves you, what does that mean if you're in a relationship?" Her father's response was immediately he loved her mother and knew she was going to become his wife. These words often played in Margeaux's mind. She had married a man that was nothing like her father. My kind of love was new to her. In comparison to how she was taught, it should be; the way I loved her was wrong.

Losing her father was hard for Margeaux, and her pain was compounded by being unable to say goodbye to him. To this day, it hurts her to speak about it all. Since she was my wife, I began to feel it was my fault she was unable to return to Canada to see her father before he took his last breath. That guilt led me to take more of a fatherly role in her life, to help her move past her pain. My advice was for her to channel her emotions into her music.

Eventually, Margeaux took my advice. She picked up a guitar, learned how to play and resumed pursuing her music. She began playing open mic shows. It was at one such event she met the guy who would later become a problem in our relationship. While she was in New York and I was still in Miami, she began dating this man for a while; I was none the wiser.

With things not working out well for me in Miami, I decided to return to L.A. to once again try my luck on the west coast. It wasn't an easy transition. I had to borrow money from my family for the trip, but I felt the move was my best chance at positioning myself for lucrative opportunities. My plans and reality didn't align, so I ended up in a similar situation as the last time I was in the city. However, this time I had a secure place to lay my head. I rented a small studio apartment in Koreatown. It was barely livable and the only furniture I had, if you can call it such, was an air mattress. I was on the computer every day reading and learning all I could. I read business books and money guides steadily absorbing the information needed for my pursuits at winning. Every day during my morning runs in Hancock Park; I would look at the large homes to become inspired.

Over time, I was able to make a little money to travel back to New York. As luck would have it, I walked right into some bullshit. I walked into our apartment to find Margeaux's email was open. Not just any emails, very specific ones. They sat there, their contents clear. What I saw devastated me. My first thought was, how could I fix this situation?

CHAPTER 3
When Women Cheat

I was in shock as I stood in front of Margeaux's computer reading the email exchanges with the guy she met at the open mic shows. The emails detailed how she missed him and couldn't wait to see him again. My heart instantly dropped! I didn't know who he was, but I knew he was able to ignite an intimate relationship with her; something we lacked for months. There wasn't any way to deny it; the emails proved they had been intimate. I was devastated. The feelings many men deny possessing, all rushed through my body at that very moment.

In my mind, I began to replay many of our past conversations. Then, I realized she insinuated something was happening. I just overlooked the signs. There was even a picture, but I didn't think much of it. I merely assumed they were only friends because often artists tend to connect with each other. The more I read, the more I learned about him. He was a participant in mission work abroad and wanted Margeaux to accompany him during his travels. I began to remember how all of a sudden she had an interest in traveling more and visiting other countries. Now, it all made sense. This man had opened her eyes to the new possibilities the world had to offer and she opened her heart to receive was she had been missing. I walked away from the computer on the first floor and headed towards the loft where Margeaux was sound asleep.

As soon as I entered the bedroom, she immediately awakened as if she knew I discovered her secret relationship. I was unable to contain what I read, so it all blurted out. As expected, she denied everything. She began explaining it wasn't what I thought and attempted to convince me nothing was happening between the two of them. If that were true, she wouldn't have told him she loved him. It was obvious her explanation was flawed and riddled with lies. Without any other defense, Margeaux reminded me of how she felt abandoned when her father passed away. This shed light on the entry point of the new guy. I wasn't there, so he stepped in to fill that void. Even after confronting her about her infidelity, I still felt like less of a man. I discovered her cheating ways, but somehow I felt guilty for not being there for her when she needed me. This only compounded my feelings about the emails. It was as if I was being punished for the constant grinding. Yes, I wasn't the greatest husband, but I hadn't cheated on her. I was all in; she was the only one I wanted and needed. After days of bickering back and forth, I ultimately decided to move forward with her as a couple. My standpoint was, women forgive men for cheating, so I should forgive her. As a team, we decided to overcome this rather unfortunate situation and move back to L.A. Once Margeaux realized I wasn't holding anything against her, she divulged everything and assured me she ended the relationship.

Once back in L.A., we quickly transitioned into our musical groove. Being with Margeaux became second nature, so it was easy to put her first again. For some odd reason, in my subconscious, I knew something was wrong. I couldn't identify the issue, so I decided to check her email again. Low and behold, my intuition didn't fail me. She never ceased communication with the guy in which she carried the relationship. Even more hurtful, the emails weren't about them at all they were about our marriage. I expected to find emails similar to ones I discovered in New York. Instead, these recent emails explained how she was pretending to get along solely for the sake of the music. I couldn't believe my wife was scheming on keeping me in love with her just so I would continue handling the business. She plotted to keep me around strictly for business while she remained in a relationship with the other guy. Once her plan was fully executed, she was to leave me and move on with him; the man she truly loved.

Once again, I confronted her about the emails, but this time it was different. I was infuriated and didn't allow her to blame me for her unacceptable actions. I didn't feel any guilt and felt betrayed because I believed she had ceased all communication with him. In her eyes, I know I wasn't the perfect husband, and she felt I was emotionally absent at times. None of that amounted her lying and cheating. Although I knew I hadn't been the ideal husband, there wasn't a chance in the world I would continue playing her fool.

Margeaux's response to my questioning about the emails confirmed her heart was in a different place and didn't belong to me any longer. She was unapologetic, defensive and offended I checked her emails again. Her concern revolved around my premise for checking her emails, not the information I discovered in them. Even after all of that, I decided to continue working on her EP. By the time we finished recording it, we both felt betrayed by each other. From my perspective, we were masking our feelings to hide how we truly felt. At the time, it seemed like the best way to display our emotions. My thought was if I hid the way I felt we could preserve her career and obtain the green card she needed. To this day, I firmly believe I sacrificed my feelings because I wasn't there for her when her father passed.

It wasn't a complicated decision to put my feelings aside and continue helping her become established as an artist. Above all, I loved her deeply and knew it was the right thing to do. For most women, one of their deepest fears is not having the person she loves by her side during the rough times. I admit, I failed Margeaux when her father died, and I never wanted to let her down again. With that in mind, I began to focus on being her friend. There had been too much damage to our romantic relationship at both of our hands to do otherwise. Years later when we appeared together on Marriage Boot Camp: Reality Stars, it was evident our friendship was the best part of our relationship. While on the show, we eased the tensions between us and gained the understanding we didn't have to be together to maintain a friendship.

Overall, I loved being married; I wasn't as ready as I thought. The most important lesson I've learned from my marriage to Margeaux is recognizing who you are as an individual before considering a union. Be sure to take the necessary measures and get to the root of any emotional scars from an imperfect childhood or previous relationship before saying "I do." How can you completely give yourself to someone if you don't know what you're giving them? The truth is, you not only end up lying to them but yourself as well.

On The Run Wasn't Just A Tour

I'd just finished recording five records with Timbaland, and on the music side, things were going well. I knew I had an open criminal case, but I had no idea it would catch up with me the way in which it did. It was 1997 and I affiliated with some guys who introduced me to a credit scam. After committing the scam for a while, I ended up getting arrested in L.A. on credit card fraud charges. During that time, I was represented by top defense attorney Angela Wallace. Once I was arrested, I paid my lawyer to ask the court to release me on my recognizance. The judge granted our request and provided me with a court date. I asked Angela what my chances of being imprisoned if I was convicted of the crime were. She explained she could have me accepted into a work furlough program because her colleague worked with the administration of the program.

I was facing five years, which profoundly concerned me because I'd started moving in the right direction. There wasn't any way I was going to prison for five years – it wasn't an option. Not to mention, I had already served a three-year prison sentence from 1987 to 1990. My attorney's goal was to secure the work furlough program for the three-year sentence instead of me serving time. When we conversed, she let me know I didn't have to appear in court. She stated she would represent the case on my behalf and assumed the judge would approve the paperwork for the work furlough program. When she arrived at court, she explained to the judge the option she'd given me. To her surprise, the judge denied her request and said, "we need him in court." Angela implied I was already in the work furlough program as the reason I was absent from my court appearance. The judge then set another mandatory court date. Once she conveyed this information to me, the entire ordeal didn't sit well, so I expressed my concerns. I told her something didn't seem right, and I felt they would arrest me during my next court appearance.

With that looming fear, I decided I wasn't returning to court and never appeared for my rescheduled date. For the next ten years, I was on the run. I would occasionally alter my name and identification card to avoid being rearrested. That plan worked, until one night it almost came to an end. I was in L.A. for the BET Awards with Manny, recording artist Keyshia Cole's manager. Later that day, music executive Mark Pitts needed a ride back to his hotel, so I picked him and his colleagues up in Keyshia's car. I guess there were too many black men riding in an expensive car because we were pulled over in Beverly Hills. Here I am stopped by LAPD in Keyshia Cole's car with my name in the system for an active warrant. I am petrified! Mark and the other passengers were oblivious to my criminal status. The officers forced us out of the vehicle to sit on the curb as two additional police cars pulled up as back up. The officers took me aside, and the sergeant asked me for my name, address, and our destination. I told him my name, but I gave him my new address. I then further explained we were on our way to the BET Awards. I figured that would explain the reason all these black guys were riding in an expensive car.

He began to ask me a series of questions as to pinpoint my true identity. I could sense by the officers' body language they knew something was wrong. There wasn't any evidence, but somehow they knew I wasn't truthful about who I was. Unbeknownst to the officers, they had a wanted man in front of them. I was indeed Londell Smith, but the address on my current ID was different than the person they wanted. The address for the individual in question was to my previous residence in LA. Thankfully, I had already stopped using that address, and I was no longer associated with it. After a few more minutes, the officer instructed me to sit back on the curb.

Mark began asking what was going on since I picked him up in someone else's car. He asked me if it was stolen and I told him it was Keyshia Cole's car. I continued to play the role that I didn't know why this incident was taking so long. After what seemed like forever, they eventually let us go with a warning to slow down even though I wasn't speeding. Although I dodged that arrest, it left me with a feeling of anxiety. I knew it was only a matter of time before my luck ran out, so I left town and went back to Miami.

By now, my attorney Angela had been arrested for embezzlement, conspiracy, and perjury. She was fighting her criminal case in court so I couldn't retain her to represent me again. I contacted another law firm and explained my situation to them. After they had researched my case, they decided to take me as a client for a $10,000 retainer's fee. Somehow, I came up with the money and began the process of maintaining my freedom. My new attorney, from the very beginning, let me know this case wasn't favorable. He informed me the presiding judge was strict and rarely lenient towards offenders. He said he would do his best to have them understand I thought everything was settled and I was ill informed by my former counsel.

The one possibility that could save me was that Angela Wallace was unavailable to speak about the facts of the case. When I talked to Margeaux, I asked for her opinion. She agreed it was time to put it all behind me. Even though, she knew it could jeopardize the music and our new group. I decided no matter what, I had to go through with it, even if it meant the music would die. My attorney was adamant about me appearing in court. He promised he would do all he could to prevent me from being rearrested. His intended defense was going to be although I made some bad decisions I was misinformed and misrepresented by my previous attorney.

As soon as they called my docket number and announced my name, the judge instructed the bailiff to take me into custody. All I kept thinking was, *I'll be locked up with gang bangers and murderers.* The judge's final words were, "you're going to serve thirty days, and then I'll make my final decision." To no avail, I asked my attorney to explain why his strategy wasn't effective in swaying the judge's decision. The judge denied me bail and stated he didn't want to reward me for being a fugitive from justice for ten years. At this point, Margeaux, my mother and all of my friends were distraught about my incarceration. I knew the type of sentence I was facing and was aware penalties could be added for jumping bail. My attorney visited me and instructed me on what I had to do next. He said it was imperative I obtained character letters from prominent people within the community on my behalf. This way, when we went back to court in thirty days, the judge could see during those ten years I was a productive citizen. I began contacting everyone---music executives, community members, friends and family members. After the short sentence had been fulfilled, I was armed with about fifteen letters when I appeared in court. The judge was slightly impressed and decided to give me one year to prove myself with one stipulation. If I committed any violations during the one-year period, I would automatically be sentenced to five years in the penitentiary. He said, "You got that Mr. Smith? I'm letting you go home, but I'm giving you a one-year probation period. If you commit one offense during this time, I'm imposing the five-year sentence. For now, court is adjourned."

I was beyond ecstatic. I didn't even go to the car when I exited the courtroom. I remember walking through the doors and going for a long walk. I felt like I had a new lease on life. If I had to serve the five years, my life as I knew it would have ended. If I had to serve another bid in prison, I don't know how I would've mentally prepared myself. All that I worked for would have suffered. The entertainment business may be full of flawed individuals, but no one wants to deal with the drama and nonsense of an artist being arrested and serving time. It prevents money from being generated, delays the process of recording and eventually destroys relationships. I knew I would regain my momentum once I was back into the groove of my hustle...that was about to get harder.

CHAPTER 4
Addressing the Womanizer

I flew back to Miami and began working with some talented producers from L.A. called 'The Runners.' I recorded a smash hit with them called, "I'm On One," which I composed for Margeaux and me. She and I were able to rekindle our relationship for a short while, but it fell apart as quickly as it started. I couldn't decipher what was going on with my relationships. Somehow, I began to feel like I couldn't hold it together. When women called me a womanizer, I understood why they believed that. However, I've always been honest with the women I've dated. I may not have always been forthcoming, but I've always been honest to a fault.

I never showed Mimi any characteristics of a womanizer. I didn't give any woman that impression of me. When I reentered Mimi's life, it was to get to know and support her genuinely. Anything that occurred outside of those confines was self-induced by her. She knew the complete breakdown of what was going on---her relationship with Stevie, his relationship with Joseline and everything else that surrounded her on the show. She had been around before and exposed to these type of situations. For the cameras, she was pretending to be naive for sympathy from the viewers. I was the complete opposite of Stevie. My purpose for coming on the show was to put her in the best light and display us as a unit. I wanted her to win so she and her daughter could be in a better financial situation.

Before Margeaux, I'd always encounter women that preferred the player type of guy. Mimi wasn't any different in her choice of men. Here I was with a woman I had a fling with fifteen years prior. Even back then, that was the type of guy she preferred. She knew how I was because we had dealings with each other before the show. Now, she can claim she wants someone who loves her, but that's not who she pursues. I take responsibility for contributing in some ways, but she was well aware of the type of guy she was dating. We didn't just meet me for the first time when we were filming the show; we were reconnecting.

I was never given the opportunity to show the side of me that had Mimi's back. I was portrayed like I was emotionally abusing her and she played into it allowing me to appear to be a womanizer. I wasn't in agreeance with her playing the victim nor did I agree to be portrayed as an inconsiderate, self-absorbing male chauvinist. It materialized that way due to the show's structure. This prevented me from showing my truths before the lies were perpetuated on television. As time progressed, I began to realize I was being used as a pawn in her game. The main issue I raised with her was how she continually allowed me to walk into adverse situations. We would have a conversation in private, once we went to record the outcome would be entirely different. If I was your man, why wouldn't you at least let me know what was going on?

I began to realize I'd done it all for her---moved to Atlanta, appeared on the show as her love interest and helped put her in a better position. That realization opened my eyes and made me accept she hadn't done anything for me. I had completely moved my entire life to Atlanta for her and the show. Eventually, it became more evident I was being used. I think people forgot Mimi was in a relationship when I first came on the show. I was pulled into a love triangle with Stevie, and he pulled her into a love triangle with Joseline. She was still dealing with Stevie, yet I was portrayed as the womanizer.

I define a womanizer as a guy who has multiple women and relationships at the same time. It's a man who deals with various women without caring about their feelings. He even overlaps his previous relationship with his new one. Even if I made mistakes with females while I was maturing, I always preferred a long-term monogamous relationship. My standard with every woman I dated has always been to have a solid foundation. If it ended, we still maintained a mutual understanding to remain friends. Guys who are labeled as womanizers think with their other head the majority of the time. For them, it's about having multiple women and multiple sex partners.

As a man with six younger sisters and one that passed away, I could never disrespect a woman in that way. Despite what you've seen on reality television, in those actual situations I would leave the relationship. That would be a conscious decision I make for myself because I'm not the way I was depicted on television. If a man possesses those character traits, then that's a different situation. You can't make excuses for a man that has womanizing ways and remain in the relationship because mostly that's letting him know you accept his actions. If you recognize it early on, you must address it and not further enable him. Once he continues the malapropos behavior, that's your cue to remove yourself from the relationship. In most cases, it's not in your favor to attempt to change a man. He has to accept his flaws and voluntarily address them, not because a woman wants him to change.

Unfortunately, the womanizing factor is now branded into reality television. It perpetuates the stereotype and places black men in a negative light. In addition, we appear to be demonizing women because it seems they can't be cordial with each other. The human mind works the same way. Perception is reality, and once you're mentally enslaved, you become physically enslaved. Black men are being shown as people who demonize women, and black women are being seen as unable to coexist.

I inadvertently played the role of being a womanizer. It was analogous to watching an old episode of Batman & Robin and seeking enjoyment without The Joker. The villain plays a very intricate role, and people want to see him in action. The viewers need the character to supply the drama for their entertainment. The show finds individuals who have certain lifestyles and they create a storyline to exploit them by sacrificing the truth. The only reason scenes were manipulated for my portrayal as a womanizer was to entertain and boost the show's ratings.

Why Men Cheat

I cheated on Mimi towards the end of our relationship for many different reasons. I'm only human and far from perfect. There's a misconception that men primarily cheat because we're supposedly unhappy with who we're dating. In every relationship, different scenarios may push a man to cheat. If it's not working and we make a mutual decision to move on; we're no longer obligated to each other. Once the love and affection are gone there isn't any need to remain together. If we've both established things aren't cohesive; what's the point in holding on? That was precisely the case between Margeaux and me.

In other cases, some men are immature nymphomaniacs. They prefer multiple sex partners rather than monogamy because they feel entitled. For many men, most likely they're not dating the one woman who compels them to say to themselves, *this is the one that's going to make me stop the nonsense.* It usually takes that one woman he realizes isn't worth losing to put monogamy in perspective. I believe if a man is transparent and honest about all the women he's dealing with, you can't classify it as cheating. Now, if he tells her she's the only one but is being deceitful then obviously that's different. In my opinion, in that case, he's not controlling his lustful desires and allowing them to control him.

Most people believe cheating is a form of disrespect, but I wholeheartedly disagree. The act of cheating doesn't determine the disrespect. It's solely about how the man values the relationship. If he doesn't view it as something of value, then in his mind he's not cheating or being disrespectful. The woman devalues herself by believing there's a chance for better treatment despite his actions proving otherwise. I feel in many cases; women accept the inappropriate behavior instead of demanding respect. This is precisely where women convince themselves they're being victimized. How can you be a victim when you willingly accepted him being unfaithful? His actions were a clear indication he wasn't monogamous, yet you remained in the relationship.

I don't condone cheating or believe any woman deserves to be treated that way. However, after conversing with various female acquaintances, they admitted to entering situations with men they knew weren't interested in a monogamous relationship. How could they expect a different outcome? If I'm given another opportunity to be married, I will not entertain another person and blur the lines. Why am I so confident? I've had my fair share of experiences, and now my values are much different. That doesn't mean I didn't have values before; it means having different life experiences puts it all into perspective. When that occurs, ultimately your values begin to shift and shape your life vision. As a matured man, now it's about making a positive impact and leaving behind a legacy. Most men have to develop into accepting this moment. It takes time because from the onset of dating very few men think with that mindset or about their future within the relationship innately.

The other aspect is many people place the blame rather than accepting responsibility for their actions. If a man has been lying and unfaithful, he shouldn't be upset when the woman he's dating wants to end their relationship. However, if a man has been dating a woman for quite some time, but falls out of love with her; he's labeled as "no good" for not staying in the relationship. It's a double standard, which contributes to a man remaining in a relationship as an unfaithful companion. The pain from the truth is understandable, but you can't fault someone for having feelings that are different the one's you've once shared.

I would be remiss to not mention my experiences as a child and how that helped mold my viewpoints. What I witnessed in both households and the interactions with my childhood friends left a negative impression. My mother never actually married my father, so I thought that's how life was intended. Ironically, all of the households in my community had the same family structure. My father lived life between two homes, so I didn't have a good example or someone to say, "when a relationship gets hard, you work through it." I'm not searching for an excuse; I'm being completely honest. Even my friends' relationships were filled with lying and cheating. Whenever at my father's house, I would witness my stepmother remain home to take care of the children while he left to commit adultery. It even affected our relationship because his behavior reminded her that I wasn't her child.

While there, she would take care of my siblings and me, yet he was out with someone else. I am the eldest of all my siblings, so I remember the experiences of a broken home. The two-parent household I had in my mind was never complete. In my neighborhood, the guys I was raised around all dated multiple women simultaneously. A few may have had a monogamous relationship, but for the majority, it was about having sex with as many women as possible. Most of my friends were focused on money and foreign cars, so women were seen as an accessory, not a necessity.

Now that I'm much older, although my household wasn't structured like the Cosby Show, I want it to function in that manner. Men are often judged by the mistakes they've made in past relationships instead of being seen as an imperfect person. Why is it that women from broken homes without fathers are easily forgiven for their mistakes, but men with the same experiences are held accountable? Men have it just as hard being raised without a father or having a strong, positive male influence. A woman who was raised with only her mother can still receive the lessons on how to value and conduct herself like a lady.

No matter how strong a woman is, she can only teach a man certain things. I give all the credit in the world to single mothers, but here I'm solely speaking about teaching a boy how to be a man. Isn't it safe to say, there's a strong possibility a child raised in a single parent home witnessing negative relationship behaviors would emulate those same actions? It's unrealistic to believe the initial thought of most men is to locate a woman he can manipulate. I believe most men enter the relationship with the hopes of being happy and satisfying the person they're dating, but sometimes he's unsuccessful.

Even with that said, I still have faith a marriage can be sacred in today's society if both individuals are "equally yoked." My understanding about that phrase is both people are obedient in the sharing of their relationship. They understand every aspect of how critical understanding each other is to their union. It's more than just understanding each other's flaws; it's about accepting them. Most importantly, it means both individuals are available to each other emotionally, mentally, physically and spiritually---it's unconditional.

Even the "love at first sight" concept can be seen in an imbalanced way, and the metrics of falling in love can often be skewed. What does falling in love mean? Did we learn each other and understand how we add value to each other's life or did we fall in lust? When this happens, a relationship loses its sacredness. If it began with a question mark, it will also end with one.

Even today, many women express how they've been hurt in their past relationships. The irony is it seems as if good women are attracted to incompatible men, and good men are attracted to incompatible women. Thinking back to when I was younger, most bad guys in my neighborhood shared the same ideals as the bad girls because they had a common interest. It's easier to be cohabitants of the same world when you share similar ideologies. Since the beginning of time, the nature of men and women has never changed.

Many men are dominant, more aggressive and looking to take charge. Their ethnicity or cultural background doesn't make a difference; men have always sought to be in control. Many women are the opposite and seek love with stability. Since men are often seeking attention from other women, it boosts their egos, which allows them to cheat without any remorse. Women can easily be faithful to a man even one below their standards because loyalty is their driving force. Men are more focused on their attention being occupied, and this displaced thought pattern leads to cheating and adultery.

When Mimi Was the Other Woman
This may sound a tad crazy, but I began as the other man when I started dating Mimi. Shortly after, I'd placed

her in a situation where she became the other woman. It was the night we were celebrating a special moment between us. We wanted to change the scenery, so we stayed at a hotel because we were always having sex at my place. We didn't book a room; we spontaneously drove to a hotel. I went inside to pay for the room but mistakenly left my phone in the car. The woman I was cheating with texted me a few naked photos while I was inside. When I returned to the car, Mimi asked, "What's this?" It wasn't as if she went through my phone; the text messages popped up. I quickly concocted a story and lied saying the girl was stalking me and wouldn't leave me alone.

During this time, I justified my cheating because in part I felt we were only sexual partners. We couldn't be seen together in public, and we were always sneaking around. There was a lot of confusion surrounding our relationship, and I believed she was still sleeping with Stevie. Actually, she was still living with him. As a result, I moved on emotionally from her before I moved on physically. I felt helpless; she was still living with her child's father and sleeping in the same bed while I slept alone every night. It was obvious they were still together, and she always had excuses as to why we couldn't see each other. In retrospect, I learned the reality TV game from Mimi, so I respected why she operated that way. However, I wasn't going to be an idiot and watch her have two sexual partners without doing the same.

I always used protection and wasn't dealing with the other woman on a committed level. She understood I was on the show and she wasn't interested in anything serious, so it worked perfectly. Once Mimi saw the pictures, I had to lie. I didn't want to ruin my chances of a possible relationship or filming with her. The woman and I had only been dealing with each other for a month. I knew Mimi didn't believe me, but she couldn't much since she was living a double life. These were the times I felt like a sucker. She would call me sometimes and say, "I can't come over tonight because he's tripping." She feared Stevie, so I had to find someone too. I wanted to be in a situation where I could feel like a man.

I didn't want Mimi to find out the truth, take it back to the show and make it seem as if I was just like Stevie. I didn't want to end up in a position where I would lose my story line. I also didn't want to hurt Mimi. I already felt bad because he was taking her through so much. I didn't want to add to her pain. I genuinely wanted to see her do better, but I was still made out to be the villain.

Making Mimi Relevant

I took Mimi from the ground floor to the top level. When I entered her life, she was presented with many new opportunities I brought to the table. Her manager was only securing walk-throughs and small photo session campaigns where she was paid with free photos and free hair. When I came in, the first deal I secured was for her to be a social media brand ambassador. She was being paid to weekly post their product. When she fulfilled that branding agreement, I connected her with an Asian businessman who owned a bunch of hair stores and nail salons. He was releasing a new nail line and was searching for a reality star to endorse his product. I presented the deal to her and explained the details. She would earn a percentage of all sales to be the brand ambassador, which would generate a significant revenue stream. Also, she would have some creative control to make decisions. We held three meetings with the gentleman. Each time her body was there, but her mind wasn't. I was the only one speaking on her behalf during each meeting, but I expected her to support my pitch by displaying her best qualities. Since she was lackadaisical and unconvincing, they didn't see her value. After the meetings, he and I had personal conversations where he inquired about her mindstate. He lost belief in her as a brand, so the eventually the deal didn't materialize.

    I added to the situation by increasing her value, so she could obtain better opportunities where she earned income. I even showed her how to outsource certain aspects of her cleaning company. I suggested she hire someone to help with the bookkeeping because her company was suffering. She was unable to give her business the proper attention it needed because she was focused on filming for the show. The person I suggested was more than qualified to assist with the problem and was able to locate an accountant to help correct accounting issues with her financial records. The individual was dedicated and ready to rectify the issues Mimi was experiencing with her business. She committed herself to shadowing Mimi once a week to learn what needed addressing, the order of importance and the plan of action. I further encouraged her to secure hospital accounts and other large accounts. Once again, she lacked the motivation to do better. I began to think, maybe she only wanted a certain level of success and was content with her status.

Then, sometimes when I presented ideas or opportunities I could feel the energy from her as she thought, *what are you getting out of the deal?* One time, she blatantly asked me those exact words and other times I could sense it in the air when we conversed. My only motive was to help her become a better person and businesswoman. My reward was nothing short of negative responses and insinuations that I had ulterior motives. The nerve of her! Can she ever say Stevie put her in a position for career advancement? They'd been together for years, but she never disclosed the root of their break up. I have no idea what happened in their relationship. She only shared with me that she couldn't find her way outside of him; she felt trapped. Everything I did was to place her in a better situation while we were together and continue on her own in the event of our separation.

I'm not attempting to take full credit for who Mimi has become. I can say with conviction; I helped her career excel in a major way. From opening her mind to view things from an abstract perspective, giving her ideas even before establishing myself in the business world, helping with her cleaning business and showing her ways to expand her brand. Remember, I encouraged her to fight back against Stevie and *Love & Hip Hop: Atlanta*. Her career didn't begin to progress until our radio interview with Egypt, which I suggested we do together. Don't paint me as a horrible person without giving me credit for the success that happened because of my vision.

Me and Althea

In 2000, I met Althea in New York City. She was living in Mount Vernon, New York and I was residing in Brooklyn. At the time, she and her ex had taken a break from their relationship. I would pick her up in Mount Vernon, and we would be together for hours. She was such a beautiful person and laid back, so it was an instant connection. She was highly interested in pursuing a career in music. Her ex was in the music industry with a major label. I thought it was quite strange he hadn't given her a record deal. When I asked her about it, she let me know working with him wasn't of interest.

We spent time together off and on for about two years. There was a lot of mutual respect and understanding, especially in the beginning because she had recently got out of a relationship. Whenever we were together, I always had to park around the corner from her house. Her mother was very strict and religious. I was unaware our families had a closer connection. I later learned my mother previously worked for her father in a bar he owned called the *Val Hal Club*. I didn't learn about this until after we moved on from each other. After quite some time, she revealed she was moving to Atlanta to focus on her music career. Later on, when I decided to take a trip down there for vacation, she let me know I could stay with her when I arrived.

By this time, she had moved on to a new relationship, but we remained friends. I didn't see her again until *Love & Hip Hop: Atlanta*. She explained she auditioned for the show, but was unable to secure a position as a cast member. It was shocking because she was living there before I was and I ended up on the show. I let her know once I solidified my position I would bring her on for one of my music scenes. Eventually, she ended up on the show as Benzino's girlfriend.

Benzino was really into Althea; unaware Stevie had sex with her. One day, Mimi came to me and stated while at Stevie's house she saw a woman there. That woman was Althea. At that moment, I didn't know she was the woman Mimi had been venting about to me. Mimi's issue was she didn't want any of Stevie's women around their daughter, which was understandable. She was already upset about Joseline being around her. The most upsetting part was, not only did he have multiple women around, but he allowed the drama to be around her as well; according to Mimi.

I decided to let Mimi know Althea, and I had sex. I felt she should be aware she and Althea had been intimate with two of the same men. Truthfully, I didn't have anything to hide. It was crazy hearing her speak about another woman Stevie and I had been with sexually. As fate would have it, years later we all connected on the show. Benzino let the world know Althea and I had sex in one of their scenes. The only time I saw her again was on the reunion show when their huge fight broke into mayhem. They originally wanted that fight to be between Stevie and I. Stevie and Joseline had so many issues with Benzino and Althea it was bound to happen.

I've had plenty of moments where women I've slept with reappeared in my life without warning. I never have time to determine if their presence will affect my current situation. Althea was the third woman Stevie, and I had shared a connection. First, it was the Philadelphia rapper Eve, then Mimi and now Althea. Although I never had sex with Eve, knowing she was very interested in us dating didn't make the situation between Stevie and I any better.

CHAPTER 5
Hard Head, Soft Heart

Many men won't admit they can be just as emotional as women. I admit I have an issue with being alone. I'm still dealing with the feelings of being with Mimi while being married to Margeaux, yet I find myself in another relationship. My most recent situation made me realize there are still things about myself I need to adjust. Why am I always attached to someone? Why do I give more to someone else than I give to myself? When I began dating Monica, I didn't have the emotional capacity to care for another woman, but somehow I ended up involved with someone again.

I met her three years before my appearance on *Love & Hip Hop: Atlanta*. It was through an attorney colleague of mine. She let me know she was representing an artist from Australia and felt it was a good idea for us to work together on her music. I'm thinking, this is an excellent opportunity to get back into the international music scene. I wasn't able to capitalize on the moment with Paula as I should have, but here I was being presented with a chance to work on music again. The challenge was, she like Margeaux, also needed a green card.

I told my colleague not to worry about it because I had an aunt whose husband worked in immigration. Because I knew someone that could help her, that's when my colleague put me in touch with Monica. I informed her that I would be able to help her with not only her music but her immigration issues as well. Upon meeting Monica, I wasn't looking at her in a sexual way. It's natural for me to help people and every woman that I've been with I've been able to put in a better situation, even if people don't agree with how I do it. Somehow, we lost touch, but three years later, we reconnected. I was wondering why Monica never took the help for immigration that I offered, but when we reconnected, it all came together. She ended up marrying someone that was able to assist her with her green card situation. By this time, I'm on *Love & Hip Hop: Atlanta* and was dealing with a lot of baggage. Monica was out in LA, and I was in Atlanta trying to make sense of all the havoc that was taking place on set and behind the scenes. I invited her to Atlanta to get my mind off of the things that I was going through personally. That's when I first felt that she and I had a special connection.

We ended up talking on the phone every day and becoming closer as friends. When I went to shoot a video for a song I recorded, I invited her back out to Atlanta to be in the video. She ended up being the lead girl, and I got to see another side of her. What I was feeling with her was similar to the vibe that Margeaux and I had when we would do a video. By now, I'm nearing my last days on the show, and things are shakier than ever in my personal life. Margeaux and I weren't getting along, and Mimi and I were done. I went out to LA and stayed with Monica for a couple of days. While I was out there, I started looking for a new home. My focus at this point was on trying to figure out how to build some steady income, and that's when things began to take off with my fitness brand.

Monica and I ended up getting closer, and when I started doing walk-throughs and events again, she ended up traveling with me at a few of those events. So here it was, I wasn't even fully out of one situation, and I'm in a brand new one, but I was honest with her. She knew everything about the show and the sex tape. She knew about Mimi and Margeaux. I didn't want to start off on the wrong foot, so there were no secrets with her. I always find myself doing business with the person I'm involved with romantically. Monica and I went from zero to one hundred with our relationship, and I went from zero to one hundred in my emotions. Things were moving faster than I had anticipated. You would think that by this time, I would assess an entire situation before proceeding forward. I'd just experienced a failed friendship and relationship with Mimi, and I was holding on by a thread with Margueax, but that didn't stop me from moving Monica out of her home and in with me. We spent a whole year on the phone getting to know one another before we moved in with each other, so I thought

I knew her well enough. I felt myself moving fast, but I still thought that I'd done something a little different this time around.

Something that would add emotional value to the relationship - getting to know her before putting all of my cards on the table. Needless to say, that thing I thought would make a little bit of difference didn't do much at all. Not long after Monica moved in, things started to go downhill. It was a blow to my ego once again, especially since I'm almost fifteen years older than her. I should've been able to make wiser decisions by now, but I didn't feel like that was the case once things immediately starting shifting. Once we settled in, she fell back off of her hustle, and I started building my fitness brand. Being in LA made me see how I could scale larger in that area, especially with the location. She ended up helping me with my Zeek Pak marketing, and I was able to see her business potential. One thing I learned from my relationship with Margeaux is that I'm not a nurturer. I didn't even realize that Monica was dealing with issues of her own and even though I'm the common denominator here, Monica wasn't ready for a relationship.

Things started going South quickly. She was trying to get my attention, but I wasn't catching on. She was dealing with a lot of darkness, and there were signs that she was depressed, but I had no idea how much her unhealed scars would end up giving me scars of my own. She told me she had some depression issues from childhood, but I would just brush it off and tell her to stay positive. I'm a guy who knows how to weather the storm, no matter how intense it gets. Most of the time, I expect the storm, and I come ready to go toe to toe with it, so I can't understand when others can't seem to bounce back after being knocked down. I'd seen strong women all my life, and even the most emotional women I know can bounce back from the deadliest of situations. I kept encouraging her and telling her that she would be fine, but that wasn't enough. The problem was, I was only listening with my ears and not with my heart.

Since I moved her in with me, I knew she depended on me for support, but my mind was heavily focused on the hustle. There was no way I was going to fail this relationship. However, to me, having money was the answer to every situation. If your stomach is full, you can focus on the other things life throws at you. Because of this, when Monica poured her heart out, all I heard was "Nikko, fix it!" I heard her, but I wasn't listening. The guy she married solely for a green card moved in with her before we got together. She eventually opened up and told me he was abusive and took her through hell. From then on, I would always look at things through the lens of trying to save her. At this point, I'd built some pretty strong connections with a few television networks, and I started looking into other ways to make money. She was a stripper before she met, but she stopped once we became serious.

For some reason, she still needed about $1,600 for her immigration. She had also paid her husband $10,000 to marry her, so she was desperate for money. Even though I told her to take some of the money I had stashed away, she still wasn't satisfied because she felt like she didn't have her own. That's when she started pushing the issue of her going back to the strip club. I didn't want her to expose herself to that atmosphere again, especially because she'd shared with me that a lot of her problems were rooted in how she felt about herself. She told me the things she had to do to get into the mindset to strip. This was when I started noticing signs of her addiction to alcohol. I knew that her going back to that kind of atmosphere would set her back, but she didn't feel like she could work a nine to five. No matter how much I pushed her to let me handle it, I couldn't stop her from doing what she wanted. She ended up taking some time away from me, and when she came back, she was a different person. When things got rough between us, she would take another break from the relationship, only to return each time as someone I know longer knew.

She made the final decision to go back to stripping, even though I didn't approve. Once again, the relationship was going downhill. I stepped my hustle game up even more and did whatever I had to do to make sure she wouldn't have to strip for long. She warned me that there would be some dark days ahead because she would be drinking just to cope with what she had to do. I would ask her how it went when she came in from her nights out, but I would try to get her mind off of it by taking her out to eat or by doing something fun, but things took a turn for the worse immediately. She started getting depressed all over again, and I wasn't able to connect with her the way I wanted to.

I began feeling like less of a man, not to mention I was dealing with my doubts and fears. We began having more conflict in the relationship because I didn't feel that I could get pass her stripping. I tried to understand her to need to be independent, but that wasn't working for me. What man wouldn't try to take his woman out of a lifestyle like that? Why wasn't Monica understanding that here in America, men don't allow their women to be in situations like that? There were cultural differences between us, but I knew our issues were deeper than that. I called my mother one day when I realized I couldn't handle it by myself. By now, Monica was drinking and handling things in an unusual manner. I've had some pretty intense moments with Margueax and Mimi, but this was something I'd never experienced.

My mom came from a place of substance abuse, and I wanted to know how she handled it. She was thirty years clean at this point, so I knew if anyone knew what to do, it would be her. My mother had met Monica at this point, and I was trying to figure out how to balance this. My grandmother was an alcoholic, and I was telling my mother how my current relationship was reminiscent of my grandmother's drinking issues. My mother's advice was to call around and see if I could get her into an Alcoholic Anonymous meeting for support. She suggested that I not tell her, but just bring it to her when I had a solution. Once I presented it to Monica, she was in denial. She said "I've been drinking since I was a kid. My mom used to give us alcohol to calm us down. I don't need help."

I was in shock. There was no way she couldn't see the problem. I was finding bottles everywhere at home - in the cabinets, under the bed and places that I guess she didn't think I would find them. She had a problem. Once I pointed that out, she opened up completely. She was introduced to alcohol at seven, and where she's from, certain things are acceptable at certain ages. I understood she wasn't born and raised in America, where seeing somebody wobbling around in the middle of the night was a bad thing. In her culture, seeing someone drunk and staggering around at night was signs of a good time. I guess just to get me off her back; she agreed to go and find a sponsor so that she could get some help.

She only went a few times, but then she completely stopped going. I knew that she hadn't been going long enough, but I thought maybe she found herself until she fell back into another depression. Once again, she started doing things to get my attention - crying, arguing about simple things and being negative. I realized I was dealing with a woman who had a sorry soul and just didn't know how to escape it. You ever have somebody tell you something, but you don't connect the dots until it's too late? I remember her sister telling me that she always had this sad countenance ever since they were little kids. At this point, that conversation was ringing loud in my ears.

SEX, ENTERTAINMENT & LIES

I asked Monica one day "Why are you always sad? What's wrong?". She started pointing the finger at me. I knew it wasn't necessarily my fault, especially since whenever she would go into spurts of sadness she would talk about what her mother and stepfather didn't do and how they had let her down.

As I thought about what her sister shared with me, I realized that Monica had always been saying something about her problems, but when you're arguing with somebody, you don't always hear what they're saying. A lot of times in arguments, you're just trying to make your point, not hear the other person out. Here it is, this girl hates her mother because her stepfather used to come in the house and verbally and physically abuse her; her biological father died from alcoholism, and her mother marries this new guy who didn't have their best interest at heart. She apparently had bottled up resentment towards her mother and stepfather. Now I'm living in a house with this broken person, and I'm trying to figure out how to fix two things - her and me. Sometimes, watching someone else going through their turmoil puts a microscope on what you're hiding.

One night, she comes to me and says, "I'm up here crying and going through it, and you aren't even here for me." I remember her walking out into the living room while I was sitting there doing some work. She kept walking around to different rooms in the house and slamming doors. I asked her a few times if she was alright and she starts telling me, "You didn't even know I was on the roof." She told me that she was in the closet shivering, crying and holding herself, and I wasn't there for her. It was like we were both disconnected and she was crying out to me, but not telling me what was wrong. I was down on my luck financially and trying to figure out how to make better moves. At that time, I wasn't trying to play Dr. Phil, but Monica wasn't processing it that way.

To me, Bonnie and Clyde means making moves and getting things done together, so you can better position yourself for the next season of life. To her, Bonnie and Clyde was me being there for her emotionally and mentally. That was hard for me to do for someone who didn't have a strong emotional and mental balance. Even if I had been there like she wanted, she still would've found an issue. The people she was having problems with weren't here with us. They were demons that she hadn't taken the time to deal with on her own. Since we were both dealing with our demons, it was like hell on wheels every day, and no amount of love, reassurance, and encouragement could help that.

I was trying to save a woman, and I wasn't able to save myself. I was still learning how to balance my life and figure out how to properly nurture a relationship, without losing sight of my role as a man. I was in this relationship for a year and a half with this woman, and I still didn't understand how I was missing the mark. One day I woke up and there were some boxes packed. I asked her where she was going and she said she was leaving. She didn't feel like she was getting the support and respect she needed. I didn't want her to leave because she had nowhere to go, but she refused to hear me out, and all she kept saying was that I didn't love her and it was too toxic for her to stay there. I thought she had been drinking again, so I tried to convince her to stay for her safety, but she kept pushing the issue, so I helped her move in with a friend of hers.

We remained in touch, and we'd talk to each other for two or three days, then we'd stop speaking for about a week. It was too much back and forth, and I just couldn't take it anymore. I had never been with a woman who was this emotional. Even my mother's pep talks weren't helping at this point. Why was it that every woman I ended up with resulted in a broken relationship that left me feeling more depleted than when I first started? There was one particular talk that my mom and I had that changed the trajectory of the entire situation. She said something that was so significant. "She's only twenty-seven. She's young. If she gets sober tomorrow, she'll be okay. You're older than her, and you need to get yourself together. Your clock is ticking. I know you want to be there for her, but she needs to get herself together. This has been your modus operandi since you were young. You're losing yourself, and you can't even make money right now."

My mother's words hit me like a ton of bricks. People think the world is dark when people are dragging you on social media, judging you based on reality television or the interviews you've done. The world can't get darker than when your mother tells you that you've messed up. When you haven't been able to pinpoint the problem, and in one conversation your mother says, "No matter what happens with the women you've been with, you will never get it right until you fix what's wrong with you." It was like I was hearing my mother's voice, but feeling my father's discipline all in one conversation. That's when I realized that I had to wake up and get myself together.

That's also when I realized that money wasn't the answer. Money was just a piece of the puzzle that could make the external part of life a little easier. Now and then you can get away with buying a girl a gift when you've messed up, but the issues with Monica, Mimi and Margeaux couldn't be fixed with money. More importantly, it couldn't fix me either.

CHAPTER 6
Sex, Secrets and the Streets

When I was a young teenager, I had knowledge about females and knew what sexual relationships were. My father was married and had four kids with his wife, but what I saw was out of balance. I wanted to have a woman by my side throughout life, but I never learned how to be affectionate toward a woman. Nor, was I taught how to love a woman, especially since my father was a misogynist. I saw him as a provider, but I also saw a man who had a skewed way of showing a woman that he loved her. Especially, since other women were a part of his life as well. His relationships were structured more like businesses.

I saw my dad take care of everything. He was the provider and was always working. He had no education, but he purchased properties and storefronts. Those were fronts for trafficking marijuana. At his disposal, he had multiple streams of income. I noticed the same pattern with myself. There he was, working hard, but only paying attention to home when he was at home. As long as there was food on the table, clothes on our backs; we were okay. He felt like everything was good.

On my mom's side, she was with the same man for years and didn't get married until I was in my twenties. As a kid, I saw him hit her a couple of times, and he called her out of her name a few time. Whenever my brother and I heard loud talking, and the arguing began, we ran out to the living room to prevent things from getting worse. The one positive thing I saw in the relationship between my mother and stepfather was that they hustled together. They sold drugs together and even smoked marijuana together. I saw a lot of the 'Bonnie and Clyde' behavior on my mother's side, and that's the perception that began to make sense. It's why I believe my relationships should operate that way.

There were two sides of my family with marriages, but it was more like a system than a relationship of love. I didn't receive the memo on treating a woman like a Queen, listening to her feelings and being there for more than sex. I saw how to work, how to earn money, and how to build a family. But, the provisions encapsulate so much more than just money. What I learned after Monica, is that its mental, physical, financial, emotional and spiritual at the core.

I never had a conversation with my dad about sex. I wasn't taught how to treat women or how not to treat women. It was on the streets that dope dealers told me there was no such thing as a soft heart. I was told to be hard and stay strong. I carry this mindset into my current relationships today. 'Get over it and get back to it' became my approach to everything. Because of this, I always felt like I had to be the man that demonstrated strength. I always wanted a woman to follow my lead and to fall in line with my mindset because seeing them cry about everything made them weak in my opinion. I was exposed to sex at a young age, so when I had an argument or negative moment with a woman I was dating, it turned into sex. That's what I was around in my circle. My friends only wanted to sleep with women and nothing more.

I lost my virginity at eleven. I was exposed to sex from the moment I could go outside with my friends. My entire existence was about dressing nicely for school to gain the girls' attention. I grew up in a life of promiscuity. I remember the times being in the house with my brother, my cousins and some of my friends. We bragged about who had more pubic hairs on our genitals. We associated pubic hair with how much sex we were having. We always challenged each other and pushed each other to get more women. The way I learned about health education was in the streets and conversations with my friends. When I attended school, I skipped health class often because I had received all the knowledge from home and the streets. The only thing that class taught me was about sexually transmitted diseases.

I realized the disconnect I had with women when I was in my nine-year relationship with my ex-girlfriend, Tavia. We began dating around 1995. Five years into my relationship with Tavia, I started dealing with this woman named Monique who was from Belize, which is located on the Eastern Coast of Central America. Even though Tavia and I were having doubts and some awful moments in the relationship; the sex was good. I knew our relationship was hanging on because of the sex. When I met Monique, we had a secret affair. Even when Tavia found out, I continued to deal with both women. Whenever Tavia and I were mad at each other, we got over it as soon as we had sex. Monique wanted to be with me, but I only viewed her as my "side chick." I did things with her that I wasn't doing with Tavia. By the time began dating Margeaux, I realized something wasn't right. I knew my emotions weren't aligned with the core values of a relationship.

Some people have parents who sit them down and talk to them about the 'birds and the bees,' but I didn't have that. I had to analyze what I was seeing and interpret it from my perspective. What I did see was a lot of dysfunction. Things may have looked a little better than the people I grew up with, but it was still dysfunctional. Much of what I saw was ingrained in guys when they are young - work hard, play harder - only the intricacies of how to do that isn't laid out. You see your father working and your mother cooking, then you emulate that same thing in your relationships.

Only now you're faced with figuring out the woman you're with while you're at the moment. Nobody expects perfection in a relationship, but most people are still trying to learn what they need while they're in the relationship, and that's what I saw growing up. My father was trying to figure it all out as he went along. Only to still have his wife upset with him. Behind closed doors, something was going on that the streets could even teach me. I was a man who knew how to take care of a woman, but somehow, I was being eaten alive by my inner beast. Although the destructive cycle started when I was a kid, I didn't see it until late into adulthood. By now, the emotional roller coaster ride is in full swing, and you can only stop it by getting off at the end. A lot of my exposure to sex caused me to end up in violent situations. Promiscuity always seemed to land me in a place of pain and a few times; it had me running for my life.

One experience I had was when I had sex with a girl who lived in Brownsville, a small section of Brooklyn. Back in those days, nobody went to Brownsville alone because of how dangerous it was. I was chasing after my dick again, and I ended up getting what I wanted, but this time it would cost me a bullet. I knew going into that neighborhood wasn't wise, even though I had my gun on me, but I just had to have this girl. I'm sure there were a million girls that I could've had sex with that day. I knew that anything could go down in this area at any given moment. Once I got there, we had a quickie, with our eyes open and pants halfway down. I hadn't been expecting anything different because that's the way it was in the ghetto. Girls weren't expecting guys to cuddle with them after sex, especially if they knew you were outside of your comfort zone. I was definitely uncomfortable being in Brownsville.

As I'm leaving her apartment, some guys across the street apparently wanted to start some trouble. I had my gun on me just to protect myself. The few minutes of pleasure I just had, wasn't worth the possibility of having to use it. They started asking me questions like, "Do you live around here? "Where are you from?" They were sizing me up and talking to me like they wanted an altercation. Once they approached me, I felt reached for my gun. They thought that they could gang up on me because it was five of them. I began backing up. I wasn't massively aggressive with them because I knew I wasn't in the best position. Although I had it in my hand, they couldn't see my gun. I was ready for anything that could happen. I was trying to get to my car, which was parked around the corner. That's when one of them pulled out a gun and fired a shot.

He was trying to scare me. But this caused me to react, so I began shooting back. I ran up the street and was almost to my car when I felt something wet in my shoe. One of the bullets hit me in my heel. I finally got into my car and drove straight home. I rushed upstairs and grabbed a towel and some ice. I waited for the girl I was dating at the time, to pick me up. We went to Kings County Hospital immediately. This was the first time I had ever been shot; I wish I could say it would be the last.

SEX, ENTERTAINMENT & LIES

The Second Time Around

One night, I was at a party and met this girl named Quianie who lived in the Bronx. She had just broken up with the guy, and I met her at a vulnerable moment. By now, this had become the story of my life. I was trying to get my life together, and I meet a girl who was dealing with a bad breakup. She was also trying to get her life together. Not long after meeting, we started dealing with each other and having sex. I was working for a firm on Wall Street at the time, but I only had the job for two months. Even though I was still hustling, the position was frustrating me. I had just closed a large deal with one of my consignment guys and secured a great connect. I had come to trust this girl to the point where she would be with me doing my drug runs and was willing to help me out if I got caught in a jam.

It was Easter Sunday, and a friend of mine decided we should take our ladies on a boat ride. I had just purchased two more cars. That day, I was driving in my BMW after Quianie, and I had just returned from shopping. We were on our way home to change our clothes, but I wanted to switch out cars first. I sent her to my friend's girlfriend's house and decided I would pick them up from there. I headed over to my mother's house alone. I went upstairs and started getting ready. As I'm leaving back out, I decide to leave my gun because it didn't feel right taking it on a romantic date. Once I get back outside, two guys approached me and started asking me for directions. The first dude asked the location of a house, and right away I felt like something was wrong.

Suddenly, the other guy pulls out a stun gun. It was broad daylight on Easter Sunday, and no one was in sight. They attempted to reach for my keys, and one of them said,"Yeah, you know what this is?!" I honestly had no clue, but I knew that they wanted the car. I remember I kept saying to myself *I'm not the guy they're looking for*. I had a feeling that someone had set me up and it had something to do with one of my drug deals. One of the guys had a gun to my back, and the other guy was in the driver seat of my car with the door closed. They kept trying to get me in the car, but I kept trying to calm them down. All I kept thinking about was my gun several hundred feet away, in my mother's house. I figured I didn't need it because I was going to be on some fancy ass boat ride, hugged up with my lady.

Eventually, I got into the car and quickly slid through to the other side. I jumped out on that side and started running up the street. The guy with the gun started running after me and firing the gun at the same time. One of the shots hit me in the back of my arm, and one hit me in my leg. I remember running through a Hispanic couple's house. They saw me bleeding, didn't do anything to help and told me to get out. As soon I left out of their house, I fainted right in front of the steps. When I woke up, I was in the hospital with Quianie by my side. Even at that moment, while I was in pain and infuriated about what occurred; I appreciated she was there for me. That girl had only been down with me on a few of my runs, but she showed how much she cared. I would soon learn that didn't mean anything to her.

One weekend not long after that, I was spending time in Harlem at my grandmother's. Quianie and I had gotten closer. Her mother wasn't home that weekend, and I told her I wanted to spend time with her. She was okay with it at first, but then I noticed she wasn't as excited as I was. Both times we talked, I felt like she was giving me the runaround, so I decided to catch a cab to her place and see what was going on. The building she lived in with her mom had a security guard, and I wasn't sure she would let me up. You could only get upstairs if you were screened in by the front desk personnel. But the guard lets me in, so I decided to creep upstairs.

As soon as I got upstairs to her apartment, I started knocking on the door and calling out her name. She kept dismissing me and telling me to go away. I heard a guy's voice in the background, which confirmed my suspicions. I was clear why she had been acting differently. I was so pissed; I kicked the door off the hinges! She screamed, and when she saw me walk inside, she ran into the kitchen. There was an island in the kitchen, and I ran around it to get to her. By now, the guy who was with her ran into the bedroom, and two security guards came upstairs to calm me down. Then, they asked me to leave. I think by the fire in my eyes they knew not to touch me or press the issue, so I left voluntarily. I was now on the receiving end of the emotional pain I had caused many women in my past. I wasn't any better than she was. Who was I to call somebody out on their morality? I was a guy who hadn't discovered how to explore his emotions, and I always ended up failing the women that I dated.

Young Nikko Speaks Out

Whenever my mother's girlfriends used to see me, they pointed out how I looked just like my father. They were always telling me how cute I was. These were the same women who would say, "he's going to be a womanizer" or "he's going to be a heartbreaker when he gets older." I saw the misogynistic side of my father more than anything else when it came to a man teaching his young son about sex and women. Even when I would ride in his truck with him, I can remember feeling like I needed to be more like him so that life would make sense to me, the way it made sense to him as it pertained to women. My life started to take that same kind of shape, only it happened quicker than I realized and I had barely hit puberty.

When I was twelve-years-old, I would run around with girls, and it was normal for me to have three girls at once. My friends and I would play hooky from school and run trains on girls to fulfill our sexual fantasies. Even at such a young age, that was normal for my friends and me. The first girl I liked and became sexual with was during the time I lived on Union Street in Crown Heights, Brooklyn. It was a girl in my building who lived on the second floor, my family and I lived on the fourth- floor.

She was older than me. My bedroom window on the fourth floor faced her second-floor window. We always talked to each other by hanging out the window at night, and that led to us making out eventually. At first, it was innocent. We fooled around and touched on each other. There wasn't any penetration involved, but we always found a way to make out about twice a week.

Around this same time, me and one of my friends would go to another girl's house after school. Her mom always worked late hours in the hospital until about eleven or twelve at night. Sometimes, we would even play hooky from school and go over to her place. Losing my virginity at eleven only caused me to yearn for more intense sexual experiences. I ran my first train on a girl when I was in eighth grade. The girl had invited me to her house one day. She wasn't expecting my friend to come with me, but I brought him anyway. As soon as she let us in, I began to set the tone. She and I had sex first. Then, he came in the room and moved in on when we were done. I waited until she was comfortable before I left, and then they did their thing. I came back in the room while they were having sex, just to make sure she was okay. Even though he and I had planned to run a train on her, I wasn't trying to put either of us in a situation where she could say she didn't want it.

This happened on several occasions with my friends and a girl that one of us liked. That wasn't the first time being with a girl, and other guys went in after me. I would go into the room and start feeling on her, and when I came out, another guy would go in. I thought this was normal for someone my age, particularly as it had been branded in my mind that females were irresistibly attracted to me. It was pounded down my throat that I would be dealing with different girls, most at the same time. I somehow was able to make the connection that my father's misogynistic ways passed down to me. It was like I'd been given an access card to do whatever I wanted. The girls were promiscuous to the point where they made it easy for guys like me, so the words that were shoved down my throat were starting to manifest in my life.

Showing Off

The showing off would continue well into adulthood with my friends and me. I remember being out in Los Angeles and the mistress of the owner of the Lakers lived out in the Valley where my girl Paula lived. Paula was in Europe at the time. I had no idea that this girl was somebody's mistress, let alone someone of that caliber. I met her while I was out grocery shopping. I exchanged numbers with her because I just couldn't let her go without knowing that we would reconnect. She had a duplex in the Valley and the first day she invited me over; she came to the door in a negligee. I had brought dinner with me, and I remember almost dropping it because she was that fine. When I first met her, I thought that she might be marriage material. I knew from early on that I wanted to have sex with her. Apparently, she wanted the same, but I didn't think it was going to happen so quickly.

We had sex on the first night, and we became close instantly. The more time we spent together, the closer we become and the more she opened up. She told me about her modeling goals and other entrepreneurial goals that she had. I remember looking around her luxurious house and thinking, *How can she afford all this stuff?* It was mind-boggling since she hadn't hit many of the goals she told me about. I finally asked her how she made her money. That's when she let me know she was romantically involved with a guy who controlled Los Angeles. My first thought was that she was dealing with a drug kingpin, but then she told me he was the owner of the Lakers.

I didn't understand why she had to be so secretive about her situation when he was married. It wasn't my place to address that. I also didn't want it to get out that we were messing around since I was only with her because Paula was out of town. Since we now had a pretty good vibe going, I decided to try my luck one night. I couldn't show her off in public, but I could certainly show her off in private. I had a friend named Mike who was coming into town. I informed him that I was dealing with a very sexy chick that would put all of our exes to shame. I sent him a picture and told him that I could get him the best sexual experience of his life. I was only showing off, not knowing how she would respond to any of it. With my friends and me, it was always about who could floss the best, boast the loudest and who had the clout to back it up.

I figured if I had this kind of game back in New York and pulled it off, then I definitely would be seen as a beast. Once he arrived, I picked him up from the airport. As we were riding back to the house, he made it clear that he didn't believe that I could make it happen. I wanted to test the limits and see how far I could go with her. I called her and told her that my friend was in town and I wanted them to meet. I even walked her through what to wear - a robe with nothing on under it, which was how she was instructed to answer the door on many occasions. When we arrived at her place, she was cooking.

I could tell by her relaxed vibe that she was open to whatever we had in mind. She was way too comfortable as if she already knew what was going on. I knew then that I could get her to do anything that I wanted. We all started drinking and laughing. A few minutes later, she and I began to make out. While she and I are having sex, she starts touching him which made his knees buckle without her actually doing anything to him. After that, we took turns having sex with her the entire night. When it was over, he kept saying, "Yo son I can't believe you got that shorty to have sex with me." And what do guys do when they feel they have something to prove? They try to see if they can get one up on you. I knew that he would try to get me laid next.

Not too long after that, I was out in New York, and at this time, my friend Mike was the manager of this hotel in the city. Another friend of mine was in a relationship, but his girlfriend had a couple of friends that were open to a good time. With Mike's connection at the hotel he worked at, we were able to book a room. We had about seven girls come to the hotel. My friend's girl was the one who broke the ice when she and her man started making out. Once she caught the eyes of the other girls, that's when all the hot action started. It was five guys and seven girls in total, and I had sex with two of the girls that night. This was a new level of an orgy that I hadn't experienced yet.

By now, this was a part of who I was and what I expected. It became the norm to have orgies, and I had a few more with Mike. All of our experiences were with women who accepted this kind of lifestyle. This wasn't about getting girls drunk and then having sex with them. We would tell them upfront what the situation would be and most of the women were into it because that's wat they enjoyed. The same things I was doing at twelve weren't any different than the years I was in entertainment. As a man in his forties, I didn't grow up hearing gay accusations because you had orgies with your homeboys who were having sex with only women. There wasn't a moment where these girls were looking at us funny because there were two guys and only one of them. Even today, I have some male friends who might call me and offer one of their women to me and vice versa. It could even be somebody that he's dating, but it's not that serious. It could be a woman that he feels doesn't understand her position. So, giving me the opportunity to have sex with her lets her know that she's just a side piece to him. I'm not saying I condone it, but to some people, this may be disrespectful. I feel if all the cards are on the table, it's honesty and acceptance at that point.

Most women that my friends and I have experienced this with were fulfilling a fantasy. They've always wanted to be penetrated by two men, and they are finally getting to experience it with no emotional attachment. When I was younger, we had challenges about who could have a female do what they wanted her to do the fastest. Whether it was having an orgy or calling another girlfriend that we could have sex with as well. It was a game to us; a game that I played all too well. As I became older, I realized those actions sowed some pretty bad seeds in my life.

ENTERTAINMENT

CHAPTER 7
Reality Television Ruins Relationships

You never really count the cost of being on reality television until the backlash happens. It's not even about the people that attack you on social media, but I feel like reality television ruins relationships itself. You appear on the shows thinking one thing, but it becomes something different. If you use Mimi and me as an example; neither of us went on the show thinking we wouldn't be talking years later. It felt like appearing on the show with Mimi tainted our relationship in many ways. It got to the point where we started looking like we were enemies, even during scenes where we were supposed to be in a good space. To this day, Mimi and I don't speak. Your life gets played out on television, and it ends up ruining the real thing you have with someone. You end up watching with the world, and you're looking at each other wondering if that's how you both actually feel.

I don't think it's necessarily the networks fault. But when two individuals go on the show, they don't always know what the result will be. You can't expect for the network to have your back. If somebody were to ask me if it was a good idea to do a reality show with their companion, I would tell them to understand they're going up against. I would suggest that they practice scenarios before filming to familiarize themselves with handling different situations. Even if you know the show's goal is to bring a certain kind of energy on the screen, don't think you have to flow with that concept. If you end up doing that, you lose all control. I believe that it's important for you to have a conversation about how you guys will maneuver to make sure you're still rock solid, once the cameras stop rolling.

If you go on a reality show with your wife, you might go on the show thinking things are okay. But if your wife takes a shot at you and you guys haven't even addressed what's going to happen when the media latches onto the story; it can seem like your she doesn't have your back. It becomes a huge competition, and the fights go beyond the show. Mimi and I would do just that. We would talk about what we would do if something happened on the screen and talk out certain scenarios. When things would change, and she shifted directions, I was in a position where I went on the defense automatically.

I always lashed back because we had a plan. Ultimately, it's the money that got in the way. If I made the most noise and people were watching, then I knew more money was going to come in. At that time, I did anything to stay in the spotlight. Reality TV is like the Hunger Games - every man and woman for themselves. There's an exception with some couples, like Rasheeda and Kirk. Even with the turmoil surrounding their relationship, they were able to bounce back because they have a solid foundation and truly love each other. There was a lot of talks, confusion, and mess before they were able to find common ground again, but they survived it together as a unit.

Most couples who go on the show are thinking about the next check. Look at Mimi and me - we have a sex tape together, we made money off of it, but we don't even talk anymore. For the rest of our lives, there will be a video out there with us having sex. My future children will see it when they become adults. Yet, I'm not even cool with the woman in the video anymore. Was there any good that came from it all other than the money?

I had a guy come up to me one day in the parking lot of Roscoe's Chicken and Waffles. He said, "thank you" a bunch of times. Looking at him in confusion, he then says, "because my wife and I made our second kid off your tape." I was blown away. Not because it feels good. But because it sucks that she and I don't speak anymore, and this tape is out there forever. Essentially, reality TV creates dividing sides, and you start believing that you have to always watch your back. It didn't ruin my relationship with my wife, but it ruined my relationship with Mimi. Some people might wonder how that could be possible if I knew I what my purpose on the show was as a love interest. Even though our relationship was built on something fake, once we started sleeping together, that created the relationship. You create a bond from there because you get deeper involved with the person. It may have started off on the note of putting two people together under the notion of getting back at Stevie, but it ended up being real.

It went well past the original thing of it being business once we started spending time together off camera as friends. Even when it came to her desire to write a book, I set up the sessions with the writer, and I made sure she was good. I wasn't even working on my book, but I was trying to help her do the things that she always wanted to do. I took boyfriend initiatives and applied myself for her benefit. A relationship that was only for entertainment purposes wouldn't have lasted. It escalated quickly into a relationship that was ruined by reality television mostly. The problem is, we let it happen. We saw it happening, and we didn't do much to try and stop it. Eventually, she fed into the misconceptions and began accusing me of not treating her right and not being good enough for her.

The other relationship that got ruined on the show was the one with Stevie J and I. I would never say we were friends, but we had respectful run-ins with each other whenever we saw each other on the music scene. Most people don't even know, but I knew Stevie J. back in 1996 when he was with Bad Boy. This was when he was at the height of the music game. We weren't friends to the point where we hung out, but we had an acquaintance relationship. We both were in the entertainment industry, and we respected each other. The partial relationship that we had could've grown had it not been for the show.

When I first came on the show, Stevie didn't know who the other man in Mimi's life was going to be. He was aware that there was another man she was seeing. Once he found out it was me, he went ballistic! He started sending her crazy text messages, and a few of them were about me. We had a few confrontations on the phone. I wanted to speak as men, but he always spoke disrespectfully. A few times, he even said things like, "I know where your moms live." He wasn't going actually to hurt my mother; he wanted me to get upset. Stevie was a text gangsta, and a lot of the stuff he said was directed at her so that I could react. She would show me the text messages. I wasn't worried, but she was, and I understood that. It was to the point where he was threatening to take her daughter from her, which people would even see from his tweets on social media.

The entire show shifted when I came in, so Stevie's presence became threatened. The show's premise was to showcase Stevie as a pimp, but with me coming on, his story line had to shift. They started putting us in scenes together so that they could capitalize off him hating me. As a person from the streets, I can say that it was a heated situation. I knew that me being on the show would automatically hurt any chances of Stevie and I being cool. But I also felt it could've gone another way. Even if he didn't want to interact with me, we still could've had respect for each other because he understands the business side of entertainment.

I even made a call to my friend Tim Dawg, who grew up in the Bad Boy world, to talk to Stevie, because I'm a street guy and Stevie grew up in the church. I asked Tim to put me in touch with Stevie by going through his manager so that we could talk and squash whatever beef we had. It was starting to feel like some real Biggie and Tupac drama. He didn't want to get on the phone with me. Around the time of my second season, that's when I had the radio interview on the morning show in Atlanta, and I challenged him to a boxing match. Craig Boogey, a good friend of Mike Tyson, was helping me put together a celebrity boxing match between Stevie and I. Even Floyd Mayweather wanted to put up money for us to fight at this strip club in Miami.

The excitement around the fight was tremendous. Contracts were being drafted, and people were betting their money on who would win. Craig Boogey knew Stevie J., and he worked on getting him to agree to the fight. For me, it wasn't about winning the match - it was about two black men making money together and killing the beef in a positive way. It never happened because Stevie decided not to do it. We could've made a lot of money off of this. We were going to be paid $200,000 each as an advance. Anyone who put their hands in the pot, including networks, had to give us a percentage, so there were upfront payment and a percentage of sales.

Unfortunately, Stevie decided he wanted an astronomical upfront figure that they weren't willing to give him. We had a chance to build off of a television show and continue to put money in your pocket, but all he saw was that I'd slept with Mimi. There were millions on the table, and we lost it just as quickly as it was offered. Not many people can say that Floyd Mayweather was willing to put money on one of their fights; even when it wasn't a real fight.

I never understood how we say we're all about our business and making money, and when the opportunity arrives, we think with our emotions. That fight would've shown the world how two black men could come together and do business during a negative moment on television. It would've shown the networks we had the control not them. We might be perceived as puppets on set, but when we aren't on the show, we control our lives. I'm not going to say that the fight had to happen for us to have some resolution, but it would've killed whatever beef we had between us.

Bloggers, Bossip, and Bullshit

Today's media landscape has changed drastically. New bloggers are popping up every day. For the last five years or so, many new bloggers see it as a way to earn an income. They aren't interested in the content or the story unless it's celebrity gossip. It's become a business and not a genuine source for people to read a great story. About ninety percent of bloggers' only objective is to build a large user base. Once they gain enough followers, they know they can get paid and begin to sell advertisement space.

Many of these bloggers don't even get the stories first-hand. They haven't put in a call to the publicist to interview the person. It's just coming up with a headline and then the content based on what gossip story you want people to buy into. The blog world has become a click game, and I have no respect for most of the blogs out there. I don't even get offended when I see my name on blogs because I understand the metrics and its intentions. Even though it's not done with quality and has no real system. It's all about finding the next story and seeing who can post it the quickest. Take Bossip for example. The whole philosophy and mission behind how it was established, was negative from the beginning. It's like a modern-day slave love letter - they created an entire entity that's meant to tear down a whole community.

There was one rumor that circulated about me being broke and getting evicted out of my apartment. I remember hearing about it and immediately getting upset, but I had no way of being able to address the rumor. I found out on the internet just like everyone else. When I arrived home, the eviction notice that was supposedly posted on my door was gone. It's amazing how far someone will go to fabricate a story on somebody. I think it's crazy that due to the protection of the first amendment, bloggers are allowed to be bullies while hiding behind a keyboard. To this day I'm leery of bloggers when it comes to interviews because you never know whether they will play or print everything that you actually said. That's why I had to tell my story, my way.

CHAPTER 8
The Mona I Thought I Knew

Love & Hip Hop was not the first encounter I had with Mona. I remember Mona from when she was with Violator, which was a management company that had Busta and Missy on their roster. She worked with Chris Lighty, who had helped me get my second deal with Sony at that time. Chris was very instrumental in my recording deal when I worked with Sony records, which is when I first met Mona. This was during the mid-90s, and at this time, Busta Rhymes and Missy Elliott were the biggest names in music. Whenever Mona and I would see each other at events or on the music scene, we would always acknowledge each other. We had a mutual respect for each other and Mona definitely appreciated me on a music level. She was well aware of my talent and what I was capable of as far as music is concerned.

I guess that's why I was so confused when Mona never once reached out to me when I was on the show. I thought that I knew Mona, but I knew Mona the music manager. Mona the producer was someone completely different. Although we weren't friends, there was a mutual respect when we saw each other on the music scene. When we did speak while I was filming *Love & Hip Hop*, it was always disconnected, and it was only in reference to the show. It wasn't on the strength of her trying to be supportive of someone that she knew and my work ethic that she was familiar with. The show was under her thumb, so whatever she passed down, that was what her show followed.

As a newcomer, I think I was expecting a warmer welcome than I received. Maybe I was expecting too much from them because I had history with Mona. My interactions with Mona felt rehearsed. Most of the time I didn't even feel like she was talking to me like I was a human being. The way things were presented to me was as if Stevie, Joseline, and Mimi were the stars of the show and I was who they had to create the character for. All she had to do now was pass that on to her staff and then let VH1 know that's what she wanted to do. Of course, this wasn't in writing, but that's the tone that was always presented in my scenes. Everyone knew that her favorite couple was Stevie and Joseline.

If you go back to the beginning when *Love & Hip Hop* started, back when Chrissy and Jim were on the show, you can start to see that an agenda was being put in place. Yandy used to work for Mona, so Mona's agenda was always to have Yandy come onto the show to ruffle Chrissy's feathers, and it was no different with the spin-offs. I thought that we had enough respect for each other that she would at least pull me to the side and let me know how things were going on. I would've been more understanding if she had said: "You might end up looking crazy, but this is what it is." It was difficult to have a conversation with her because she wasn't on my team. I remember bringing her about twenty ideas showing her how I wanted to present myself on the show.

When my father was deported to Barbados, I asked them if we could go down and film something there. I asked if my mother could come on way before they eventually let her come on, but they never let it happen the way that I wanted. When I submitted those ideas to the producers, they took them, but I knew there would be a protocol because Mona had to approve it. Once the mandate comes down from Mona, they ask you to submit your story line and then it's shaped from there. However, one of my story lines was accepted until the sex tape came into play. Even with the ideas that I sent in, they didn't shape anything around them.

By my third season, they started allowing me to record things at my house, but it still wasn't until my wife came onto the show. I don't think the viewers even noticed that I was always in Mimi's shadow. I remember running into Mona at an event in New York where we had a conversation about my career. Mona asked me what was going on with my music. We touched on it briefly, and I remember saying "When I get some things going, I'm going to call you." She said "Okay. You have my number, just call me." Somehow, that call never happened, and it's not because I didn't have anything going on with my career. I just ran into Mimi again at a time that was perfect for Mona and the show.

Today, I think Mona is all about exploiting the talent and letting the talent fight through their issues on television. But I'm pretty sure they aren't fighting the way they would if the network hadn't shaped their story. Of course, she can always say that she isn't exploiting anyone and that she's only providing a platform. I think she took the platform and started thinking, "Hey, these white people trust me, and I'm going to do what I need to do to make sure they continue to trust me." The creators of the show was a white guy named Stephen and his partner, which was another white guy. As I think back, I can see how even with the fight we were supposed to have how the network may have manipulated the outcome. I went out and dropped soundbites about how I wanted to challenge Stevie to a boxing match. It permeated the urban sector, but then it vanished. I think the network saw how that fight could jeopardize their franchise player, which at the time was Stevie. That's how it all works. If someone sees their key player being jeopardized, they're going to step in, whether it's in government, sports or entertainment. If I would've won the fight, then Stevie gets embarrassed, and the show has to find a way to make him look great again, especially since I was the villain.

One talk I can remember having with Mona was in the third season, which was my second season. It was our most intimate conversation to date. This was the first time she ever came in to speak with me on this level. She came into my dressing room to speak one-on-one, but it still felt like it was to set the gauge for the reunion. She said, "you're always ten steps ahead" and then reminded me to be in the moment. Her approach came off like another hustle move. I didn't take it personally, but I had nothing left to give to her at that point. That last scene where Stevie and I were about to fight was the one time that she was heavily involved in any of my scenes.

I also realized that even when it comes to the pieces of your life that you don't share with them, you end up having to wonder if they'll find something out and surprise you on the show. In my opinion, the network had to know I was married. The day it came out that I was married, I was at Margeaux's interview for immigration, where she was about to get her green card. Either *Love & Hip Hop* knew this all along, or somebody saw us going into the immigration building and made a call because when we were done the interview with immigration, the story was all over MediaTakeOut.com. Margeaux started snapping at me like I was the one who had told them. It could've messed up her chances of her getting her green card, so she was wondering why I would say something, but I didn't. She thought I let them on it because they caught the story at the moment when immigration was interviewing her.

Now I look like a guy who is leaving his wife out on a limb. That's when I started to realize that the show would get it's story no matter who got hurt in the process. They didn't care whose life would be negatively affected. After leaving the show, I felt like people hated me for sure, especially the producers of the show. I can be at the airport or at a restaurant and people will come up to me with accusations. The network made it clear how they wanted me to be perceived, and people bought into it. Even though Stevie treated Mimi horribly, he was being seen as somebody that needed to come to her rescue, and I was the guy she needed to be rescued from. More than anything I think people hated the fact that I didn't fight back. Because I wasn't saying much, it was almost like an admission of guilt, as if remaining silent means you're guilty. The few times I fought back were almost pointless because no matter what I said, the people heard Mimi louder.

Staged Fights With Stevie J.

Most of the scenes with Stevie and I were staged. In the scene with Stevie and the watch, we were having a single release party for "NY to LA," the song I did with my friend, Johnny. I was under the impression that the show was giving us a single release party, but it ended up being a facade to benefit the show and the ratings. Mimi showed up with her friends, but I didn't get the memo that Stevie was going to be there, but I later found out that Mimi knew. Stevie walks in, and the first thing he addresses is the watch that she had on her arm. I should've asked Mimi why Stevie was there, but I didn't. The producers told me that he was coming in, but they wanted me to let things play out between him and Mimi, and then he and I could talk.

They had it set up so that we were far apart at the table and that there was enough security around. I knew that it was staged when he said something about the watch because there was no way he could've known about the watch unless someone told him in advance that it was a gift from me. He didn't ask her where she got the got the watch from; he just started calling her out on it. When he insinuated that it was ticking, even though it wasn't, that's when we exchanged words. The one thing that people don't get to see is the stuff that happens naturally to cause you to get upset or get into a fight. Mimi and Stevie knew about the scene, but I didn't. Since I felt blindsided, I immediately went on the defense. That was when I called her 'damaged.' While she and I are exchanging words, Stevie grabs her hand and takes her outside to a brand new BMW, which was rented by VH1 and went back the next day.

I even noticed how they both had on all white. If it was not planned for him to show up, how could he have been dressed in the same color as Mimi? They never showed the viewers the part where we lunged at each other and almost came to blows. They just gave him the upper hand and made it look like he was the man. They set it up so that it looked like Stevie came to save the day with a BMW when I only gave her a watch. Each scene was crafted to make him look like he was always the one on top and made me look like I was a sucker that wasn't on his level.

The second fight we had was when I was coming out of the gym. It was shortly after Mimi and I had a discussion about her book. When I came out the gym, Stevie was looking down from a balcony as I was walking to the parking lot. That's when he said "keep my daughter's name out your mouth" and started going off on me. They had a few security guys there, and I knew if I would've walked down the steps, security wasn't going to let us fight, especially since each time I tried to walk toward him, they always stopped me. When I saw the window to get over the balcony, I took my chance and tried to kick him.

I was on the balcony and security pulled us apart on separate sides. They asked us to finish out the scene, but he ended up walking off. He tried to act like he was walking back toward me, but security kept pushing him in the other direction. Even though Stevie and I didn't have a lot of scenes together, the ones we had were always explosive. This is when I should've realized that this was all a setup. How could it be that a lot of the scenes he did with Mimi were calm, even if they had started off arguing, yet, every scene I'm in with him, there was fighting and yelling?

I knew that saying "your daughter's going to be calling me daddy" would piss Stevie off. Reality television is all about wordplay. They want to see who can get their words out the quickest and who has the slickest one-liners.

Of course, I said that to get under his skin, but they were looking for more intense scenes between us. That's the kind of stuff that they needed to know - what can you say that will get him the most upset and vice versa. What they forgot to consider was how it would play out in the street even after the show ended. I have no idea what would happen if Stevie and I saw each other today. I know that because he's still in his ego, a fight could go down today if I see him. Not because I'm bitter, but I know that there's still some tension there. We haven't seen each other in public yet, and we're talking about three seasons of heavy tension that has never really been addressed, especially since it ended on the note of the sex tape with Mimi and me.

Stevie and I have had mutual friends before *Love & Hip Hop*, one being Eve. When I met her, I was living in The Hills out in LA, and this was right before she got signed to Ruff Ryders. I had a red two-door Benz, and I went to this club on Melrose Avenue. When I put the top back on the car, I saw her coming out of the club. I knew right away who she was. When I hopped out my car, I walked over to her and introduced myself. We started talking and eventually, we exchanged numbers. We never hung out, but we always talked on the phone. I had so much stuff going on, that we never got a chance to hang out, even when we would make plans.

The next time I saw her, it was in New York with Swizz Beatz about a year later. We were in front of Sony Studios on 54th Street and 5th Avenue. When I pulled up, I saw Eve in the passenger seat of Swizz Beatz car, and we reconnected again. At this point, I've run into her a few times, and I can tell we're still feeling each other. I had been in New York for awhile at this point, and I ended up going to a party. I ran into Eve at the party, but this time, she tells me that she has a man. Then one day, I was in Mr. Chows on 57th Street in Manhattan, and I ran into Eve again, and we embraced. That's when I saw Stevie behind her. My friend that was with me noticed how Stevie was looking at me with fire in his eyes. I think that was around the time all the envy started. Here it is, he and I were never really that close, but I had talked to Eve before they got together and now, we're on a show together where I'm dealing with his child's mother. He also knows that I used to mess with Mimi long before the show. I believe there was some envy there and some underlying hatred for me. I'm not even sure if he knew that I used to talk to Eve, but the bottom line was I had connections with two women that he loved.

About a year after that, I called Stevie up and told him that I thought it would be a good idea to start a group. I approached him around the time he and Puffy were having a disagreement, and I suggested we come up with a group named Celebrity. It was me, Stevie, Mario Winans and Bryce, a guy from Groove Theory who would make up the group. Bryce agreed to it, and even though Stevie wondered what he was going to be doing, I knew he would fit perfectly. Mario Winans, however, opted out. He was working with Puffy at the time, and I don't think he wanted to be in a group. I was trying to recreate what I had with Flirt, but once again, it just wasn't working out.

Whatever idea that I had back then about Stevie and I doing business together could never be rebirthed. I think he proved that with the celebrity boxing match we were asked to do. Our relationship on reality television has created a permanent dent in whatever chance we may have had to build a musical relationship or any relationship for that matter. I can't put the blame completely on Mona, but I can say that the Mona I thought I knew was now a business mogul who was more concerned about building her franchise then giving people a platform to tell their truth.

CHAPTER 9
Half-Scripted and Half-Reality

The truth is, no one forces you to do anything in reality television. However, they do interpret it in a way that makes you feel like you're being controlled. There's an undertone in the show that makes you feel like you can't say or do anything that they haven't cleared. You have to look at it in two tiers - there are truths behind the scenes in one tier, and there are flaws in the other tier. The flaw in reality television is they have to control the set and the talent; they have to control the scenes, the timing and the climate in the air. Everything that's being controlled in that sense is being controlled by the producers and the staff.

For example, if you have Lisa, Mike, and Jenny and they all know each other, they'll have scenes together or scenes where they end up referencing each other. Let's say Jenny tells Lisa about a conversation that she and Mike had at dinner the other day, but Jenny doesn't tell Lisa everything she told Mike and some of the stuff she tells Lisa, she didn't even say to Mike. So if Lisa goes back and now has a conversation with Mike, she's giving all the information that she has, which to some extent may not be all the pieces that he hasn't even heard yet.

Now, let that come into play in a scene: you have it where Jenny and Lisa are having a conversation on a whole new day at a different location. If Mike pops up on the scene, he's coming in with a chip on his shoulder, and with all the information he got in between his conversations with both ladies. He thinks Jenny lied on him, so now, he has to defend himself. That's where the scripted part begins. There's no one answer when it comes to the question is reality television real or scripted. It's about how you look at it. When a lot of it is staged for you to walk into situations where you are questioning someone, you may not know that well, or you're questioning a conversation that you only have limited information, yes, it becomes scripted. Real reality would be me having a camera follow me around in my everyday life so that even if there's a substantial amount of editing, people get to see my truth. I might have very few issues with what they may see because I know that either way they edit, what is on screen happened in my life.

To get the ratings they want, producers have to find a way to manipulate the talent. It's still willingness because you know what's going on and that's never hidden, but a lot of it has to do with producers asking the right questions and knowing how to put the show together in a way that suits their vision. You have to remember they aren't dealing with actors. With scripted dramas, actors understand they are under control in a sense, but it's for the sake of the art and the character they are portraying. A director will yell cut a hundred times until he feels the actor has it right. In reality, you aren't dealing with actors, so the producers have to find something to stretch and do it, so the talent doesn't feel like they are being manipulated.

There were a bunch of scenes that they wanted me to do that I was completely against. There were times we had to work out the scene in a different way because I just wasn't going to do it. At some point, you've got to be in control of your story, even if it's just a little bit. I get the entertainment factor, and I don't knock them for it even if I don't particularly care for the way it's done. Some people have asked me if the producers should ever pull the plug when it goes too far? It depends on how you look at it.

I know people will ask why I did it if it was so contradictory. To be honest, I stayed because, by my third season, I was trying to see if I could redeem myself. I didn't take a lot of what happened on their personal, so I never looked at it like it was contradictory. It's like a double-edge sword. The sword is sharp on both ends, but it symbolizes both the gift and the curse. When you're swinging the sword away from you, it's the gift, but you can end up using that same sword to cut yourself if you end up swinging backward and that's the curse. In reality, sometimes you get thrown into situations where you end up swinging backward unintentionally, but you realize it only after it happens.

Either way, I chose to use it as a tool and make it work for me. I stayed on the show strictly for business. Once you learn the game, you learn to play on your terms. You may not go into it with that mindset, but you end up seeing what it's about and you take it from there. People jumped on the bandwagon of this fictitious image of Nikko. Necessary evils are important to entertainment today, and even someone with the squeakiest image can be made out to be the villain. I learned that the only way my story line could live was if I was the character they wanted me to be.

I spent most of my life being the villain in the streets, so it was something I knew best. There are parts of me that have villain traits. I didn't understand why they couldn't use parts of my real life to get their villain story line. They didn't need to paint me as a womanizer. I would've been more receptive to them painting me as a male whore. There's plenty of drama to be found in the truth. I value my sisters and my mother. I grew up in a city that doesn't tolerate men disrespecting women, especially during the time when I was growing up. If you want to pull the bad out of someone, you don't have to lie on them. We all have a story that can make people turn their heads in shock. So does it mean that every man has to be a womanizing bastard to have a great story? Or that every woman needs to be this broken creature that has no concern for her body and just goes through men in crazy cycles?

SEX, ENTERTAINMENT & LIES

Entertainment is all about having a strong story because that's what gives you substance. We just live in a culture that has to be the first to tell the story, even if it's not all truth. Once I saw the pattern of how the show was taped, I felt like my truth could've been told, and the results would've been better. Some people needed a story line, but I already had one. That's not to say that I would've put my whole past on television, but there were ways to get the drama needed without making me look like I have no respect for women. But I get it - the villain is the heartbeat of any great story. It's all about the way it's presented in each sector of entertainment. People have come to enjoy when rappers have beef, the drama on reality television and the 'skeletons in the closet' concept. We've watched the villain concept since the days of Batman & Robin. The only thing that has changed is the internet. By the time an episode airs on Monday, I have ten seconds to go on social media and try to defend anything that was on the show that wasn't true or that didn't show me in the best light.

The world doesn't give you a chance to catch up to what they believe. How can you catch up if, while the episode is airing, you might be taping another episode or even the reunion? Then you hop online and realize that only a fraction of what you taped got aired. You know that each episode will be edited and you know that each episode won't get everything in that you said (they can't even do that with a movie adapted from a book), but to edit to the point where the truth looks more like a forced lie on every episode is disturbing. Then, add to the mix that you only get 140 characters on Twitter and have to write a book on Instagram just to say "this is really what happened." That's time-consuming and draining, and there was no way I was going to do that every week. The way the producers would set up the questions was to make you think that you were in control. They would ask you the same thing a bunch of different ways to portray themselves as honest individuals who are concerned about telling your story correctly. I never had the chance to hang out with the other crew members, so we never got to exchange notes. There was always a respect for one another, and we were cordial when we did see each other, but I was only close to Mimi, so I didn't have the opportunity to build relationships with other people on the show the way everyone else did. I always feel like I was slighted in that area. I also didn't get the feeling that I could use the *Love & Hip Hop* platform for my music. I had recording deals with Sony and Epic Records, but nobody ever talked about or mentioned that. There were a few times I was in the studio, and they filmed me and there were times we talked about music, but it wasn't in-depth the way I would have liked it to be. Even Jim Jones was seen performing and in the studio all the time.

After all this, I wouldn't necessarily say that I'm the most hated man in reality television, but that was the way I was viewed. I also know that's what some people are saying. Since the show didn't cater to my music journey, I figured I could make this villain thing work to my advantage, so now, I'm having fun with the whole villain concept. It's one thing to say something on the internet or to create memes bashing reality stars, but a lot of people don't even know you, yet they think you're best friends when they see you in the streets. One time I was at a restaurant in Atlanta with some of my friends. A girl came up to me and asked me if I could take a picture with her friend who was celebrating her birthday. A few minutes later, I had another woman come over to me and say "why did you do that to Mimi?" and all I could do was laugh.

The woman who approached me was someone who appeared as she carried herself with class. I made her step back and think about her question. How can you fly off the handle and ask me a question about something you saw for a few months? Everybody forgets about the moments in between, the moments before and the moments after. Unfortunately, along with people asking can they take a picture with me when I'm out, you have the people who stare at me in disgust. My worst fan reaction was the time I was out in New York with my friend, Brasko. We saw a car ride past us. Once we caught up to the car at the light, the passenger side window rolls down, and this girl sticks her head out the window and starts shouting at me. She's calling me all kinds of names and telling me that I'm a horrible person for doing what I did to Mimi. I couldn't believe that this car full of girls was stopped in the middle of the street in New York. I remember snapping and going off on them, but Brasko was the one that reacted. He quickly came to my defense, and all I could do was shake my head and laugh as I watched one of my closest friends almost make the girl cry. If this were what my life had become, I would be getting into a lot more arguments.

Opportunist vs. Hustler

These are probably two of the most interchangeable words that I've ever known. Somehow, people confuse me with being an opportunist. In my opinion, an opportunist is someone who looks for circumstances and gains something for immediate advantage. In some ways, we're all opportunists, but I'm not an opportunist regarding how people think I am and to be honest, it's not necessarily a bad thing. It turns into a bad thing when you're an opportunist, and you end up taken advantage of someone.

A hustler is a go getter, someone who works harder than most to get sometimes bare minimum results. Take *Love & Hop Hop* for example. When they were at the hotel sizing me up and showing interest in me to be Mimi's love interest, I took the opportunity. I became an opportunist by taking advantage of the moment. The hustler mentality kicked in when I started taking other opportunities and trying to figure out how Mimi and I could keep milking the moment. After *Love & Hip Hop*, I went back to look for opportunities and was figuring out how to hustle them. If you look at it from the other angle, *Love & Hip Hop* was all about opportunity as well.

The show seeks out individuals who are broken, have a story and are looking for a memorable moment. They just do it in a manner where they exploit you and show you the way they want to show you. Most of the time, black people love to exploit each other, while white people sit back and watch and take advantage of the moments when we're at our weakest. With black people, we don't know how to get the money together, and we spew so much hate toward one another that we can barely build together. A black A&R rep at a major label might be quick to give a white artist an opportunity instead of a black artist because he believes he already knows what he's going to get from the white artist.

People are always going to question black people. If we take the white man out of the equation, there's still questions and concerns when black people are involved. When I was coming up in the hood, white collar crime was way more respected than blue collar crime. If you did a white collar crime, you were seen as a genius and praised for being able to do something so conniving, because white collar crime is more organized. Blue collar crime - robbing stores, doing stick ups and selling certain kinds of drugs - is what where many inner city black men lend their focus. I grew up in a system of blue collar crimes. Because of where we come from, most white people don't respect us from the minute they see us. We still disgrace our women, pull each other down and treat each other with no mercy. When I think about the whole Illuminati concept and how our culture constantly throws someone in it once they become successful, I think of the crab basket mentality. Why is it that when one of us starts to get rich, become successful and more influential, we automatically viewed as devil worshipers or that we have to be in some secret society?

The Illuminati concept is nothing more than you becoming a master in your field. When you start to sit with billion-dollar players, people will accuse you of being in this secret society, but people's perceptions of the Illuminati is twisted. It's simply another meaning of power. You're basically at a level of such power that you can get anyone on the phone, and you possess a certain kind of knowledge in life. This group has been around since before the 1500s. Blacks are just placing each other in the category without even knowing what it means.

It's similar to people calling me an opportunist, but they have no clue what it means. You may not even know how to spell the word 'opportunist,' but you heard someone else say it and now, it sounds good. The reason why it's taken out of context with black people is that a lot of what we're seeing black people accomplish has never been done on this level before. You have blacks making millions like never before, and for some people, there has to be a reason. We just can't be this smart or this gifted and make this amount of money, but why can't we?

SEX, ENTERTAINMENT & LIES

Love & Hip Hop | Season 2

By the beginning of season two, my first season and Mimi's second, Mimi and I were at an all-time high, both personally and professionally. Our minds were caught up in the Bonnie & Clyde moments, and we were very comfortable with each other. Mimi had become more comfortable moving on from the whole Stevie and Joseline situation, and I was settled into our affair. I trusted in the security of our relationship, and we had become a celebrity power couple. We were being requested to do appearances as a team, to travel to different cities and make money together. I remember feeling the same way I did when I had music being released. I was on cloud nine, enjoying the attention and the perks that came with the lifestyle.

We were being asked to make appearances together, show up at clubs and we were building together to the point that both of our teams knew each other well. We were having house parties and having events at each other's homes. I was there for her when her father passed away, and she had met my mother. The show didn't seem to understand that we were heavily moving like a power couple, even when we weren't being taped. By now, we both had one foot in and one foot out the door. I could still feel the negative undertone dealing with her, and it started to look like I was her hoe. She was still dealing with Stevie, so it came off like she was having her cake and eating it too. It started to feel like I was working for her, especially because in most cases, she had the upper hand. Mim's attitude started to shift. She was acting like she was entitled to the way I was treating her and helping her win.

We saw each other every day, and we moved like we were a full-time couple, not a couple who was just on a reality show. We had two different mindsets when it came to how we worked. Her mindset was one of waiting for the show to call and tell her when she had to work, but I didn't come from that. I wasn't waiting for the show to give me a vision for my life. That's not to say she was, but I think the difference in how we moved made it feel like the relationship was slowly moving like a business. She met my mother and most of my family during the second season, so it was real. It was even more real during my third season, but that's when I started to feel like we were losing momentum.

Love & Hip Hop | Season 3

After season two was over, neither one of us knew we if we were coming back to the show. In my opinion, there was no real reason to bring me back because we gave so much in the second season. We went into season three knowing that we had to have something strong to have a solid story line. That's when we thought of the sex tape. I knew that I needed Mimi for certain things to get done as far as the show was concerned. They knew that they could control me by controlling Mimi because they couldn't control me by themselves.

SEX, ENTERTAINMENT & LIES

At this point, I was thinking about a solution. I knew that there was a chance I would no longer be on the show, so I was thinking of the next thing I could do to make sure I had something solid to leave on. The relationship between Mimi and I was shaky, but I was still trying to hold it together. She was feeling broken, and she also had no idea what she was going to do, especially since the show wasn't sure about our stay. When it comes to the sex tape, I had never done anything like what we did before, but I was with it, and so was she. I knew if we were going to do it that we had to support each other all the way to the end.

Part of the reason why we didn't just say we had a sex tape, even though we knew that it would've been good content for the show, is because it would no longer make her look like the victim. She couldn't go from playing the victim to now being willing to showcase a sex tape. She was the one who suggested that we come up with something to make it look like the tape was leaked. When we cut a deal with the President of Vivid, Steve Hersh, VH1 didn't know anything about the sex tape at this time. Vivid wanted to do the deal with us and not Viacom, which is who owns VH1. I started thinking that it would be a good idea to bring VH1 into it. I knew the marketing landscape would work having both of them behind us, but again, we lost some of the control. That's when Mimi started acting differently. She started distancing herself from me, and I could feel that something was about to go left.

Mona manipulated the whole play with me looking like the guy that leaked the tape, but Mimi was okay with it. At that time, Mona and Mimi weren't even getting along. That's when my marriage was brought up. I would go to ask Mimi out, and she would say 'no.' I could sense the difference in her aura. She started making excuses whenever I wanted to be together. I called up one of my friends and told him that I though a shift was taking place. I remember saying to myself, *Something is going on and Mimi is way too relaxed about this sex tape situation*. I knew there would always be some hesitation, but she went from being super concerned and shaky about the whole concept of the tape being released, to being too comfortable talking about the tape. She went from asking me questions on how to handle interviews about the sex tape to being more confident.

Even though Mimi was acting differently when it came to our personal relationship, our professional relationship seemed to be going well. Mimi and I had the power couple walk through of life at this point, so I started to put some things together. Our minimum rate for both of us to appear was $6,000, and we were doing two to three appearances a week. I had a lot of respect for her, especially since I wouldn't be on the show if it weren't for her. Because of that, I wouldn't even take half the fee, because I knew that she had a price before I got on the show. However, it was guaranteed that we had to be booked together. For the first couple of weeks that we tried it this way, she was with the idea. After about a month, she completely switched up on me.

Her manager's phone was ringing off the hook again, and things were looking better for Mimi on the money end, so her manager was ready to take me out of the equation. Her manager would be on the phone with my agent, making it seem as if she was with the whole set up, but she always had Mimi's best interest at heart. The problem I had was that Mimi should've had my back. She could've told me that she was thinking of doing things differently. We had already done a few gigs together as a power couple, but her manager was able to convince her to do it solo. When she started doing events alone, people were confused. They would see Mimi booked by herself for ten dates, so whatever memo we had put out that we were supposed to be doing things together or you couldn't get either of us, had become null and void.

I had a conversation with her about why she would allow her manager to book her by herself. Her explanation was that those were dates already set up before our sex tape and before we agreed to do things as a couple. Because I she was getting caught in a lie, an argument would ensue. Even with all of this, I still wasn't catching on to everything that was taking place. At this time, Margeaux hadn't been brought onto the scene yet, and she was upset that her name was out there. Margeaux isn't the thirsty type, so she was confused as to why her name was going around on the blogs and how she got brought into my mess. She was working as a bartender, and she's truly the girl next door, so nothing for her is ever about money. She didn't like what was being said about the sex tape or us as a couple. She came on the show for two reasons: her first reason was to defend herself and the second reason was to vindicate my name. She wanted to let them know the truth about the sex tape and the other things that were being said about me that were false. Margeaux was upset with me, and we weren't even together, but she felt the need to come out and speak on my behalf.

The Shift

Mimi decided to stick to the dates that she had and didn't continue with what we were working on as far as appearances. That's when I felt that things the way I knew them to be were coming to an end. At some point, I think Mimi started to believe that I leaked the sex tape, even though we came up with that lie together, she somehow starting believing her lie. We agreed to do this, and we both came up with the plan, but Mimi can be easily persuaded. She started believing what the public was saying. By this time, Mimi and I were on the opposite ends of the table. She went all the way left with the hype around the sex tape. I saw her go from being a frightened woman with no direction, coming to me and asking me how to do things, to her not needing me anymore.

We were still filming, but at this point, we had stopped talking and seeing each other off camera. We were only talking for business purposes. When people were asking her questions in the press about me leaking the tape and making me out to be a womanizing dog, she never said anything. I knew then that we were both bitter towards each other. I was bitter that she had thrown me under the bus, but I didn't think she had any reason to be bitter because I'd always had her best interest at heart. She was ready to confess, but she was telling everyone that she knew about the tape, but that I had leaked it. I don't think anyone believed her at this point. She was saying that I was the mastermind but also saying that she knew about it.

We came up with the sex tape plan together. I didn't hold a gun to her head, and I didn't threaten her to do the tape. She was at the table with me when we talked to Vivid Entertainment. I was confused as to how she could tell her friends on the show that I did it, but then turn around and say that she knew about it. At one point, we both had an interview with the same magazine at different times. She went first, and in that interview, she stated that she was in on it but that I created the whole plan. Now, we're at the end of *Love & Hip Hop*. The tension between her and I is so thick at this point that you could feel it whenever we were in the same room. My last full conversation I had with Mimi was in a scene taped on the show. The show wanted me to show remorse and apologize to Mimi for not telling her about my marriage. I apologized for the part I played in that, even though I stand my ground that if my wife and I understood we weren't together, why should anyone else need to be concerned.

Once Mimi and I stopped communicating with each other, I felt no need to tell her I wasn't coming back to the show. The only person I needed to talk to was Mona and her business partner. I'm in a position now where I don't even have any love or respect left for some of the producers of the show. I can understand that they had a job to do and were just puppets themselves. The plot was created for me to be the villain and that's what happened. By now, since my wife had become a part of the show, as well as her girlfriend, there were hints of us coming back. But when Mona and I talked, I told her I would be out in LA. They hadn't opted to bring my wife back yet. They wanted her, but there were some things she was on the fence about in regards to the contract.

When I got the call, I made it clear that I was not coming back to Atlanta. That's when they pitched me *Love & Hip Hop*: Hollywood. They asked me if I wanted to be on that show since they would be filming in a few weeks. I approached them with some conditions of my own, so that this time around, I could play my hand better. It was a new city, new contract, and a new show, so I wanted to negotiate my pay. They weren't in agreement with my numbers, and I wasn't in agreement with theirs. At that point, I made a decision not return to the franchise. Two weeks after I had decided not to do *Love & Hip Hop*, WE TV called with the opportunity for me to do *Marriage Boot Camp: Reality Stars*. The call came through one of my associates, and he told me that they wanted me to do the show. I hadn't talked to Margeaux for two months, so I asked him to speak with her and to get her on board first. Once she agreed, I was excited to do it. The entire show was taped in three weeks, and I was able to get what I asked for as far as pay. I had made the right decision not to return to *Love & Hip Hop*.

From Hip Hop to Boot Camp

Marriage Boot Camp: Reality Stars was taped in three weeks in a large mansion in Beverly Hills. The way the crew and network handled business was totally different than what I had experienced before. The business atmosphere was completely different. I felt like *Marriage Boot Camp: Reality Stars* gave me an opportunity to rebirth Nikko London. I didn't expect to go on a marriage counseling show and try to work out my marriage problems. I didn't know anyone in the house other than Margeaux. Her girlfriend was furious that I was even on the show, but the deal was for all three of us to be there. I thought I would be uncomfortable trying to work out my problems in front of a bunch of other couples, but I wasn't.

I wasn't sure how either one of us would react or how she was going to handle things. We hadn't been around each other since being separated, and we hadn't lived together in a long time. There were so many unanswered questions about our marriage that we hadn't been able to work out on our own. It was an opportunity for people to see us in a different light, but it was challenging. We were open to doing it because we knew it could be good for business. The show is presented like we were a group of individuals who were brought on the show to be rebellious against the counselors. At this time, Margeaux and I were trying to figure out how we could do this without tearing each other apart. I was trying to figure out how we could be in the same house again for that long without hurting each other even more. We had a lot of resentment towards one another, and we had pretty much brushed all of our problems under a rug. Margeaux was trying to decide between her girlfriend and me, yet we still hadn't put all of our issues out on the table. As the show progressed, we all started to see how the counselors were making sense and that if we took what they were saying into consideration, we could grow from this, whether we stayed together or not.

Marriage Boot Camp gave us an identity that *Love & Hip Hop* didn't give us. We were humanized more with this show. I saw more value in this situation than in the one with *Love & Hip Hop* because I was able to see the flaws and things I needed to improve on. The show even allowed me to see other relationships and see that we didn't have issues that couldn't be healed. Seeing those other couples and how they talked to each other, dealt with each other and made each other look crazy on television, allowed me to see how Margeaux and I could at least save our friendship.

SEX, ENTERTAINMENT & LIES

However, Margeaux's girlfriend presented a problem for me. When I was going through the problems with Margeaux and the other guy she was seeing, she would tell me every night when she would come home after work about a gay girl she knew. I never realized that something was going on, but she would always say that she thought the girl liked her and she would tell me how the girl always made her laugh. I would ask her questions and joke with her about what they did each night at work. I had no idea that at the time, she was talking about Merika, the girl she's with now. She was trying to let me know the whole time, but once again, I wasn't paying attention.

Once I came on the show, Merika hated my guts the moment I walked in the door. She's Russian, and she doesn't speak clear English, but one thing she made clear was that she was going to be hostile toward me. I understand that she loves Margueax, but the show is called *Marriage Boot Camp*. Why wouldn't she think I would be there? When she saw that there was one room for all three of us to sleep in, she took it hard. I was cracking a lot of jokes and having fun with the whole situation, but she was snapping and making it seem like I didn't belong there. I was more lighthearted on this show, and I was able to have some fun. The negative exchanges between Merika and I would increase because she felt like I was in her way and Margeaux wasn't responding to me the way she wanted her to. Eventually, I sat down and got to know Merika, and I realized that we have a lot of things in common. With Margeaux and I, we realized we were together for the wrong reasons, and we're now at a place of peaceful reconciliation. We're at the place of being able to get along, and I'm genuinely happy for her. We still have each other's best interest at heart, and we're able to coexist and maintain a mutual respect for one another. I wonder what would happen if all reality shows cared enough about the cast that they could have peaceful reconciliations. But I guess it wouldn't be called reality television.

CHAPTER 10
The Musical Genius

On both sides of my family, I was exposed to great sounds and tunes long before I even realized that I'd be in the music industry. To say music runs through my veins is an understatement. My mother always played oldies when I was young. The Commodores, The Delfonics, Patti and all the other great soul artists that came up during that time, helped shape the sounds I grew accustomed to infusing in my music. I discovered my love for music during the time I grew up hearing the guys I liked such as Big Daddy Kane, LL Cool J, Nas and Jodeci.

My father's side was where I was introduced to the West Indian culture and Reggae music. He's from Barbados, and whenever I had a chance to listen to those sounds, it was like capturing a piece of my culture. Since I got the soul music from my mom and the reggae from my dad, I was able to fuse the two, but I discovered gospel music on my own. I got turned on to Commissioned and Men of Standard, who were great to me, and I could see how their flow was influencing many R&B groups. When I was studying the craft of music, I understood then how a lot of people emulated the greatness that was already out there.

Surprisingly, I started rapping before I started signing. When my brother and I used to be in the hallways in the projects, we would just start rapping. We would bang on the walls and come up with beats. Even on the streets, we would find something to bang on, and we'd find ourselves rapping and coming up with some pretty dope music. It may seem like people from New York automatically find themselves involved in music, and that probably has a lot to do with the entertainment blood that runs through the city and the birth of Hip Hop in the Bronx, but it was something that captured me from day one. I could've chosen any other path, but music honestly chose me.

From there, I was exposed to the nightlife and being out at clubs opened me up to dancing and how important it was to music. Once I started going to church and listening to particular choirs, I became more engrossed in the gospel. By this time, I was fusing rap and singing but primarily found my way back to singing. In the early 90's, I befriended some guys, and we ended up becoming a group called Flirt. Everyone had their flow, and we got along pretty well, so we ended up renting out a brownstone in Brooklyn. Since we had the entire brownstone, we took advantage of the space and had rehearsals during the day and parties at night.

It worked for us because we were huge sex symbols. Even when I think of what Hollywood did by bringing *The Get Down* to Netflix, I find myself reminiscing on my musical journey that played a significant part during the 90's. I'm not saying I started anything, I'm saying my musical talents and contribution, even behind the scenes, was a huge part of the musical era back then. I didn't have anyone influence because I was truly a student of the art. I wanted to learn the best music in every genre and a lot of the legends like Marvin Gaye, Donny Hathaway, Bobby Womack and Sam Cooke, really made me appreciate the art. I was like a sponge and could learn something from anyone doing great at that time.

Music played a huge role in my life when I was a kid, even when I wasn't singing or rapping. When I needed to escape from things like my mom arguing with her boyfriend or an issue that I had to face head on, I would turn on some of my favorite tunes and just go somewhere else in my head. Even today, I like to create the kind of music that makes people forget about their everyday struggles and go on a musical vacation. It also played a big part in me surfing through the streets. Without music, I don't know how I would've survived. I'm infused with music, and in a lot of ways, it helped shape my style and how I carried myself when I hung out.

One of my go to records was always *Change Gone Come* by Sam Cooke. There was also a record by The Killers that whenever I heard it, it would immediately lift my spirit. It expanded my imagination and allowed me to stay in my creative process. You can always find something that helps you set your barometer, even during a crazy time in your life. I could hop in my car and take a two-hour drive and come back feeling better because I had the right music playing during my ride. I always listen to songs that can take me where I need to go mentally. Today's musical landscape has changed drastically because you have to be more than an artist today. You have to be a businessman as well. Jay-Z understood that very well, and that's why he's where he's at today. Diddy and Master P. all had that idea that they were dealing with something bigger than the music. These are guys who came up during my era, so even during the seasons of hardship that came during my earlier years as an artist, I had a different mindset.

It seems like nowadays, a lot of artists are satisfied with the craft part, but haven't gotten completely acclimated to the business part. Being a starving artist is not easy. You will have your doubtful moments, your depressed moments and your stressful moments. I don't think there's anything positive about being a starving artist. But there are two kinds of starving artist - one has no plan of how they are going to get their music heard at all, or they play to the closest congregation of who is around at that moment; the other kind of starving artist is the one with a vision. The starving artist who has a vision still has a steep road ahead, but you just have to stay ready and be prepared for the moment when your season comes. You keep building, and you understand that it's not just about creating and performing music - it's about creating a career of longevity and something that will sustain you over time.

SEX, ENTERTAINMENT & LIES

It's just like the difference between the person going to college who has no children and the one going who does have kids. The one who has no children can go full-time and knock out her degree in four years. The person with children may have to go part-time because they're focused on taking care of their family and going to school. It's not impossible for them, but it becomes harder, especially if they're working. The landscape changes and what would've taken four years may take six, or more. The person without children, even with difficulties and challenges arising, can get through those four years and smash it.

I think every artist has to go through a down time that almost makes them want to give up. This puts them in a position to work harder and learn how to put together a strategy. I was fortunate enough to have other ways to provide for myself. Because I was seasoned, I always understood that having a solid plan was just as, if not more important, than having solid music. You have to study what you need to study so you can be better than the next person. It's difficult being an artist, but you have to have a strong vision to pull you through the difficult times. The key thing to everything is your imagination. You can't let the fear take control of you or lack of money be an excuse not to move forward. It doesn't take money to do music - it takes money to sell it and to get it out there. The focus is what breaks most people because if you can't focus long enough to execute something, then you'll always be falling backward.

NIKKO LONDON

Even when you think of what's going on in Los Angeles now - it's like a modern-day Gold Rush. Things are permeating here like they did back in the seventies. It's too many artists now, and a lot of them are very talented. I see the starving artist thing a lot here in LA. Nowadays it's harder for artists to make money because they don't know the business. It's paramount for artists to know the business more today than the craft. The craft has gotten watered down, so you have to get in line with having an income and understanding the business side of everything, but most artists don't have that because they rush to get the check and they don't learn to appreciate the process of learning the business.

Not to mention that today, it's all about streaming. Some artists are streaming one song but making millions of dollars off of that one song. It shows they understand what's going on, regardless of how old they are. Because I worked in music during the nineties, I have an advantage that a lot of newcomers don't have. Even with the changes in technology, I can still find my groove and catch what's going on now. I have to understand what's going on in music now and learn what I like to keep the flow of my music career going. I always find out what's going on currently, and I find out what I like in all genres of music. Once I find out what I like, after mixing it all up, I go from there. Most people do it the opposite way, and they look at it like they can't compete or keep up with the younger artists. In their mind, they're stuck in a time warp. I look at it like a captured moment. My life is always being captured in moments, so I stay on top of everything that's current, from fashion to music. This is why I always talk about how important imagination is. If you can use your imagination to see beyond what's currently happening, you can move in ways that help your career. Why hate the younger artist or hate on what they're doing? Think in the current and find a way to flow with the best of them.

My biggest pet peeve is when people ask me how I'm going to keep up with the new stuff today or they question why I'm still trying to make music. I immediately shut down on people like that. If you're not savvy enough to figure out how to capitalize on a moment of change in music, you'll always be behind, or you'll always end up making excuses. I don't get caught up with the age thing. Some older guys are so intimidated by the younger guys in music that they talk bad about them instead of figuring out ways to learn from what they are doing. Staying current means learning new things and engaging with new people. So many people are afraid of knowledge, and it affects how they do business as an artist. Everything has already been done before, so you have to find a way to do the old while adding something new to it.

If I could go back and hit the reset button on my musical journey, I would tell myself to learn the business first. A lot of people get weighed down with their craft, and that's what causes a lot of people to lose love for the craft. All we had in New York was creativeness, so I had no excuses to find a way to get to what I needed. I grew up being creative, and I hung with guys who had the crazy ability to come up with ways to get things done. Growing up in a city where people took trash cans and banged on them with sticks to create music, there's no way I couldn't do what I needed, even with no money. Although pursuing music can be a lonely journey, music is half of who I am. I have no idea where I would be without it. Only you know what you possess inside of you, and you have to get people to see the vision you're trying to birth. I always say you can't force a connection and sometimes, you have to walk the journey alone to get to the point where your vision starts to grow and expand. It's not about isolation; it's about understanding that not everyone will get it; not everyone can flow with you or help you with the manifestation of your dreams, even if they say they're interested in doing so.

    I believe that I'm a musical genius because once I jump into music, amazing things happen. The truth is, I don't always feel like what I do is the greatest, but people have always shown me love for my music and name which has made me appreciate how others sometimes viewed my work as genius. I do music on a level that makes sure I'm competing with what's out there. There's not a lot of people that can do what I can. Some would argue that anyone who calls themselves a musical genius means that person has a large catalog of published work. To some extent, that's true, but not in all cases. Some people put out albums, but that doesn't automatically make them a musical genius.

What makes me a musical genius is not about me being cocky, but appreciating that I've had longevity in this industry. It may not have been in the form of a full album, but I've worked with Timbaland, Tamia, Gerald Levert and was on a label with Aaliyah and Tank. The fact that I was a part of music with geniuses like that and had the privilege of creating music with them is what makes me a musical genius. How many people can say that they've been making music for twenty-something years with no album but has credibility in the business? There are a few, but I appreciate that I'm one of them.

I wrote a song called *On My Way* with Tamia and Track Masters, which appeared on her *More* album. I also did a song called *As A Child* with Rick Ross, but not a lot of people knew about it. You can Google it now, and it'll come up on YouTube, but what people heard and seen me on television didn't give me the opportunity to showcase any of my musical contributions. This was ten years ago, and Rick Ross was just beginning to build his name in the game. This was right around the time when his song *Everyday I'm Hustling* was very popular. We connected after he told me what his fee was for laying a hook. I got the money together, and we made it happen.

What's missing to me as far as a connection to music, is the way people today are getting started. There's a strong generational gap today in music. I started in the era of the demo, so going out, beating the pavement and talking your way into music made sense. So many artists who came up with me were true hustlers, and if there were issues, even when it came to beef, it was about the business and money, not because of a chick or because we didn't like each other's label mates. The foot groundwork for the new generation is so different from the foot groundwork of the old generation. In fact, today that kind of application doesn't exist. For my generation, we had the best of both worlds. We can learn and maneuver the social media and tech space, but we know how to hustle and how to navigate the business socially - very few in the new generation have that.

They may know the tech space and how to build digitally, but they struggle with having meaningful conversations with people in business. How can they have a meaningful conversation in business when they can't even have a meaningful conversation with each other? I may not be as tech-savvy, but I can pull my way up and figure out the part I'm missing. There is a different temperature that's going around, which doesn't necessarily make it horrible. A lot of artists in today's music game that are doing well aren't even appreciating all of what the music business has to offer.

There's also a disconnect with the way people connect behind the scenes and face to face. In my day, we appreciated the building that took place - building relationships, connecting at parties and giving people a chance to see you in your element, not rushing to success or calling something successful that's not. When artists choose to take their time and craft their projects, they can make moves in a way that fits their vision instead of the vision of a label. Artists need to learn the business quicker today and technology has made that easier. If you aren't taking advantage of that, then who can you blame?

CHAPTER 11
Production Hell, The Worst Times in Music & TV

In the entertainment business, production hell can be very tough. To create a great song, it can take a long time to bring it together. If you have five writers, then you have to get signatures from everyone involved, you have to reach out to each publishing company and get the necessary permissions to distribute that song. Then, there's mastering, engineering, writing, and coaching - and that's just for one song. It's all about creating a great feeling with the song. After I'm done my part, I have to send the song to someone else to master it, which can take even longer. The artist may want the song in a certain time frame, but that doesn't mean that's when it will be done. Production was always an up and down situation that artists never have control over unless you're doing each part for yourself. Guys like Pharrell and R. Kelly do everything themselves, but they have a lot of skin in the game. With a new artist, you have to work around everyone's schedule.

The first deal I ever had was with a group called, Flirt, which was a four man group. At the time, we were a

Tri-state sensation. It was in 1992, and at that time we had a deal under East West Records, which was through the division that Sylvia Rhone controlled. We were just a group in the neighborhood that was ready to live our dreams and Sylvia was able to help us get with a label in Japan. The guy who invested in us was Jerome Sydenham. Carl Thomas also had a group at this time, which was before Bad Boy records, and that's how we met. We teamed up with his guys and different guy groups at that time, doing different shows and traveling across the East Coast.

This was also when the male groups Shai, Jodeci and Silk were making a name for themselves. We never got a huge name like they had, but we were popular in our area. The label we signed to ended up getting their label dropped by East West Records, which ultimately affected us. We no longer had a deal, and we were back at square one. We started to have disagreements, and we ended up falling out because of all the egos in the room. Even though we had worked with Track Masters, Mike Warner and other major producers at that time, we weren't able to keep the group going when the business side started to fail. One of the biggest things that we did was go to open mics about twice a week and perform, which helped us to get our names out there. Performing at open mics helped pruned me for the career I would eventually have.

There was this one club in New York City called, Chaz & Wilsons, which was on 79th Street and Columbus Avenue. It was one of the most popular spots during that time. It was a restaurant and premier place for artists to perform and you had to have some name just to get in. The more popular it got, the longer people had to wait in line to get in. Another popular spot was called, Sweet Waters. Being in places like this helped me to soak up great music and take the time to learn from other artists. I met my group going to places like this and we were able to connect with a lot of musicians and producers. Michael Speaks, a good friend of mine who sounded like John P. Kee, started to make a name for himself quickly. He came to New York homeless, but he had a seven-octave range that people fell in love with immediately. He had five companies that wanted to give him a deal at one point. Once he got a deal, he bought a house in Brooklyn. We became really good friends, and I learned a lot from him, even though he was a gospel singer. He was the one person you didn't want to perform after during an open mic night.

What I learned from him showed me that Flirt still had a long way to go. We were still trying to figure some things out as a group. We pulled Jerome Sydenham in to manage us, but we thought it would end up being a conflict of interest. We decided to speak with my dad about managing us, and he agreed to do it. I saw my father manage my two brothers and my little cousin, who had formed a rap group called The Rugged Ones, so I knew he would be able to help us. Since he managed them, I told him to speak with Jerome and see if he could get my brother's group over here with us, but before we could start working, my group decided they didn't want my dad to manage us because it would be a conflict of interest.

I didn't want to give up so easily, so after a few talks, they decided they would give it a try. Everything was going well until he started paying more attention to The Rugged Ones than our group. I eventually ended up firing my dad. We were trying to find a label at this point because we had a name and we were pretty well-known. I guess the time frame and the way everything was playing out caused us to have more tension, and the egos got bigger. That's when I decided to go solo. I hadn't thought about it, but it started to make sense. We were bumping heads about how we were going to maintain our rent and bills. Things were shifting, and we all started thinking about going to get jobs. We had reached our lowest point, and between all the fussing and arguing with the guys, I was trying to stay focused. That's when I met a girl named Paula Brown.

She was the first girl who had ever brought me out to California. She was a dancer for Alvin Ailey Dance Company, and we met at an open mic night. As we started to get to know each other, the group started to disperse at this point. It was perfect timing because things weren't going well with the group and nobody knew what was next for us and how we were going to make ends meet. She told me she had a house in LA and she invited me to go out there with her. Nothing was happening in New York, and I wasn't leaving my dreams

NIKKO LONDON

up to a group, so I said yes. This was in 1995. Once I got settled in LA, I learned how she was a huge success in Europe. She ended up singing lead for a group called, Snap. She started giving me advice and even suggested that I put something together for the group she was singing with in Europe.

I had never touched the international music scene and only had a background in R&B, but I decided to give it a try. Paula began to show me an unfamiliar life. I didn't have a passport, so when she was traveling to Europe, I ended up staying back in LA. I took advantage of the art scene out there and began to learn the music business. I was taking charge of my career in LA meeting different people and putting myself in the music mix. I became friends with Allen Payne and reconnected with my New York friend, Tyson Beckford. I had a slight burn out from music and ended up dabbing in the theatrical world, but never really took it seriously. With acting, the wait is hard, and I wasn't interested in waiting for my number to be called.

Seeing Tyson made me recall a time that he and I had a small disagreement back when we were living in New York. There was a guy named, Rick, who used to hang with Haitian Jack, someone who ran with Tupac back in the day. Somehow, they had bumped heads, and I was trying to explain to Tyson that he didn't want to go there with a guy like Rick, but Tyson wasn't backing down. Most people saw Tyson as a model who was cocky. Because I was trying to mediate between the two of them,

Tyson looked at it like I was on Rick's side. Once we reconnected in LA, we reconciled whatever differences we had in New York, and I started to hang with him.

I was doing okay in the business area, but the longer Paula stayed out of town, the more I had sex with other women. That's when I made the decision to get my passport. Mission Control, one of the largest European booking agencies, was backing Paula at this time. I went out to Europe to spend time with her. Once I got there, it was the first time that I was able to see how valuable she was to everyone in Europe. I didn't know where Paula and I were going to end up, but I wanted it to work out because I knew that we could grow together musically and personally.

Eventually, the Hollywood lifestyle had taken me by storm, and I needed to get back to my roots of music. When I got back to LA, I set up a meeting with this producer in a studio. As I was walking down the hallway, I ran into two guys who were twins, and they heard me singing. Their names were Stacey and Tracey Brandon, and they were from New Orleans, and they had a deal with Atlantic Records. They had a group called The Real Seduction, and they were in a position to call the shots with their group. I started hanging with them, and one night, they had a show at a church and asked me if I wanted to join them. This was right around the time I began to get back into gospel music and was into the group, Commissioned. They were able to get me back into the mix of music, even though I was doing mainly background stuff. The more we hung out, they became like my brothers.

Around the same time, I had recorded a song for this group, and it ended up on the soundtrack for the movie, *Sprung*. Quest Records, which was Quincy Jones label at the time, had the soundtrack and the song we did was called, *Let Me Know*. I was working with this guy named Kyree who was the junior A&R for Quest Records. I ended up meeting Jay Brown, who is the current manager for Rihanna and Kyree's brother. It seemed like every connection I was making wasn't leading to longevity and I was working hard. With all the work I had been trying to do musically, I ended up getting burned out, so I headed back to New York to regroup. I may have sown my seeds in LA, but the harvest came when I got back to New York.

I landed a writing deal with Case. That came about through a gentleman named, Kenny Smoove, who's the CEO of Sporty Rotten Records. Case was signed to them, and they had a deal through Def Jam. Once he found out I had the writing deal, we started working out of Homeboy Studio, a popular studio in Manhattan. Kenny had rented out the studio to work on Case's next album which I ended up working on. I came up with three records for Case, and two of them landed on his project. Because Case was such a major artist, I was becoming cockier and thinking that I was untouchable. I was also still making moves in the streets. I wasn't sure why, but I knew it wasn't the smartest move since things were going well for me in the music business. I decided to go back out to LA, even though I was knee-deep into recording my album. I think being home in New York was too comfortable for me. For whatever reason, I didn't even push the album that I was working on. I had the connections and everything set up, yet something was still missing. So I decided to return to New York again. This time, with a purpose to fulfill.

I came back to New York and landed my first solo deal with EMI records. Lindsey Williams was the president for EMI, and he wanted to sign me. The music I had done with Case had caught his attention, and he was ready to help me become a full-time artist. D'Angelo was on the label as well, and he was at the height of his career. I did my first single, which was *Why Do Girls Love Harder Than Guys*. Gerald Levert was the writer on the song, and he had sent the record to BMI with his reference. Darren Grant, a film producer, was given his first chance to produce a music video for us. As soon as my single was about to come out, that's when they sold the label to a publishing company.

I was being managed by Eric Nicks, and I was able to get out of my EMI deal. Somehow, Lindsey Williams and I became friends, and he took a hiatus from the music business. Eric Nicks was a friend of mine that was working for Violator Records as an assistant to Chris Lighty. Eric Nicks was climbing the ladder and was making a name for himself, which was how he ended up managing me. The news starting spreading that EMI had sold the company and was now a publishing company. It had already hit the tabloids and the papers. Eric started working hard on my behalf, and Chris Lighty took an interest in my deal due to Eric's prodding. I was sitting in Chris's office, and he ended up putting in a call to Sylvia Rhome. She immediately showed interest, and he walked me up to her office. She was ready to make a deal.

Tim Dawg was the Vice President of Epic Records, and the President was Ron Sweeney. Tim was the person who discovered me when I was going to do the deal with Sylvia. By now, I had two deals on the table, but Sylvia's Elektra Records deal came in later. The numbers were better with Epic Records, so that's where I signed my deal. I ended up recording a whole new album and did a majority of my album out of Sugar Hill Studios in Jersey. I rented out the studio for $80,000 for six months. Because of all the new recording that I was doing, I didn't use the songs I did with BMI. I wanted to do a whole new project with Epic and bring something different.

I was in the studio every night, and I started to feel like I was back in step again. Just when I started to get into the full swing of things, they fired Ron Sweeney. The new president, Dave McPherson, came in and decided to clean house. He was coming over from Jive records and coming into this new company; he brought all his people with him. Once again, I'm back at square one. I was beginning to feel burned out again from the music industry and decided now was a great time to go back to LA. Eight months later, I signed another deal with convicted drug tafficker Jimmy Henchman, who had managed The Game and Brandy. He was also behind the deal that I had gotten with Black Ground Records. I had already failed three times with music deals, but not a lot of people can say they were able to keep getting a new deal after not having much success with the others. I wanted to make sure I capitalized on this opportunity better than I had the others. I was beginning to feel like my time in music was passing, but I knew that my gift was making room for me. It was like every time I signed a new deal; God was telling me He had something better planned.

Role Models in Entertainment

Talking about all the opportunities I've had in music and even the more recent ones on television, I have to address the reality that most role models won't be found in entertainment. I didn't set out to be a role model, and I'm sure VH1 never had that in mind. There was something that Joseline said on the reunion show of my last season that struck a nerve. She said that it was horrible that I didn't have children at my age and because of that, I must be gay. Being forty-something and not having children should be applauded. I'm working hard every day and trying to build something for myself, even if people don't agree with the way I'm doing it, yet I'm being judged for not having babies all over the place?

The sad part is, it's a stigma that's become so widely accepted, and people think when you aren't like everyone else, then something must be wrong with you. Stevie has multiple children by different women, yet he's the one you're comparing me to? I'm not passing judgment, but I'm realistic. She was viewing things as a Latino woman who just stepped into a black world, yet her point of view is jaded. She thinks that it's normal for a guy to be like this because she's experienced in men. In my opinion, at some point in your lifetime, at least one person should want to be you. I don't think anyone is walking around that says "I want to be Stevie" or "I want to be Joseline." Whether it's your niece, cousin or somebody following you on Instagram, somebody should want your life. If you don't have that, then how can you ever question anything about anybody else? I'm not saying that people should turn into you, but your life should be admired to the point where someone would feel like being in your shoes would make their life better. Most of the people on *Love & Hip Hop* were being judged, and people felt bad for them. They may have received some love, but is it genuine or based on whether the fans like you this season?

My role models growing up were Berry Gordy and a lot of the business guys that started something from nothing or who had their company. They had ownership and were able to capitalize on their music business and pioneered a lot of what we have as blacks today. In my opinion, they showed us what it was to build something and own it. The landscape of role models today are nowhere near what I grew up seeing. The floor is open for anyone who has an imagination. Even with people having their landscape, there's nobody doing anything original. We lack great leaders today, and we aren't able to see individualism like we did back then. The influence of today is rooted in rebellion and people aren't thinking about the generation behind them. Everybody is running under the same metrics, and people aren't thinking about the direction in which people are being led. It's almost like the blind leading the blind. People are afraid to be different and say anything against what's trending.

For example, they asked ASAP Rocky about Black Lives Matter and what he thought about the shootings. He said he lives in Beverly Hills and what he sees is different. He wasn't necessarily speaking against it, but he asked, "What happens when blacks kill blacks?". I agree with him, but the tabloids got a hold of it and made it seem like he was against the movement because he lived in an affluent neighborhood. They also made it seem like he was selling out his community. He tried to clean it up, but by then, it had already gone over people's heads. Our community doesn't know how to agree to disagree without tearing each other down. If you want your children to have role models, it starts at home. If most of the parents today were fully present in their children's lives, would they even know the details of my life or have time to read about the latest gossip? Reality stars and celebrities lives will always be up and down, and most of what you see isn't always true. Your child's greatest role model is the person who they see every day and who they depend on to make things happen for them day in and day out.

CHAPTER 12
Memories in Music

Some of my fondest memories in music were the ones that were behind the scenes. I was in Biggie's *One More Chance* video, which was an honor in and of itself. Everyone that was hot in music at that time was in the video, so to be among them was a big deal. I was also able to hang with them after the video. I was able to make the moves I was making and hang with Bad Boy because of my friend, Tim Dawg. The video was done in Manhattan in a brownstone owned by a female friend of mine. Biggie and I both grew up in Brooklyn, and that's how I knew him. I grew up in East Flatbush, but moved to Clinton Hill later on, which is where Biggie was raised. After the video shoot, we all drove down to D.C. to hang out.

Years later I would regroup and connect with Bad Boy again in 1998 when I worked with Shyne, who would later go on to be known for his involvement in a 1999 club shooting. I met Shyne when he was young and hanging out in New York City. I had done some time in the jail with one of his uncles. At this time, Manny Halley, Keyshia Cole's manager had a barbershop and

NIKKO LONDON

Shyne used to hang out at the shop. I remember him rapping for me, and I wanted to see what he could do in the studio, so I asked him to come down. That day in the studio, there was me, Shyne, Eric Nicks, Sugar Bear and a few other heavyweights in the business. Once he was done rapping, I realized that he had a great flow, but he didn't have a strong structure. I asked him if he was familiar with eight's and sixteen's. He wasn't and even said he wasn't really into that. That's when I realized that he was strong with rapping, but he had to learn how to flow and pull it together in music. I broke it t down to him on how to break things down with a hook and how to write bars for the business. We talked about what he needed to do to bring it all together, and he ended up learning quickly. He got so great at it that he ended up with several deals on the table. Eventually, he went to a bidding war with labels, and he ended up signing with Bad Boy.

I think it was a good deal, but the wrong deal for him because he and Puffy clashed. I was there when the shooting broke out at the club. My friends and I were all at the club on 43rd Street. Shyne was with Puffy, Jennifer Lopez and Wolf, who is now deceased. Scar, who was a street guy, was also in the club with his guys and their table was right next to Puff's table. Somebody in Puffy's crew was throwing something up in the air. Scar and his friends were throwing things in the air as well. At some point, it all caused a commotion. There was an exchange of words and Shyne got caught up in his ego and pulled out his gun. That's when everything went down, and shots started ringing out in the club. People started running, and everyone got scattered. Of course, we all know now the details of that incident, which resulted in the high-profile case with Puffy and Shyne back in 1999.

My next memory in music happened with someone who had become a good friend of mine. It was December 2002, and Jennifer Lopez was doing her video for *All I Have* with LL Cool J, who I had met through my manager Eric Nicks. LL had heard my stuff one day at the studio, and he wanted to meet me. He was looking to sign me as his artist and with us both being into fitness, we were also working out together. I would go to the gym with him and his trainer, but it was hard for us to work together musically because I was coming in second most of the time, especially since he was an artist himself. The biggest thing for me was that he appreciated my music and what I was doing at the time. He told me to find a song he could jump on, so I did, but again, we couldn't bring things together to do a deal. He didn't have the time to nurture his label, but we remained friends. We had a strong bond, so when it came time for the video with Jennifer, he asked me to be in it.

I also had a connection with rap legend Foxy Brown. I grew up and went to school with a guy named Don Pooh. And at this time, Foxy was the female threat in the game. She was coming in strong, and her songs were filled with lyrical content. Don had a barber shop on Washington Avenue, which was around the corner from

Foxy Brown's house. I put a bug in his ear about Foxy, because he didn't know who she was at the time. I was pretty cool with her brothers, and I let him know that she was definitely somebody to watch. When he asked me how she sounded, I played a little something for him, and that's when he wanted to meet her. That's how she came into the game and got the deal, and Don Pooh ended up being her manager. Pooh was able to get her on The Nutty Professor Soundtrack. Then, she did a song with Case, and everything blew up from there. Pooh had made enough moves for Foxy that she had a bidding war on the table.

I always looked at Foxy like a sister and my friend Don Pooh was managing her. One night, I went to her crib to hang out with her, and we went and grabbed something to eat. Her song Ill Na Na had just dropped. We were sitting in her truck, and she was telling me about her boyfriend and all the troubles they were going through. One thing led to another, and we ended up having sex. I wanted to know whether what she was saying in her song was true and now I know that it is. Later on, when I got on *Love & Hip Hop*, Don Pooh and I would reconnect when I asked him to manage me, which he ended up doing for a season. We had been friends for so long, yet hadn't ever worked together, and I saw this as an opportunity for us to do so. Little did I know how much of my entertainment days would end up reflecting on parts of my life that had already happened.

SEX, ENTERTAINMENT & LIES

Entertainment Mimics Life

Being a kid in the streets of Brooklyn, I wanted the lifestyle that I'm now living, but I was doing it in a way that wasn't legal. I had a spot on Madison Avenue, and this particular day I had several kilos of drugs coming in. I took the initiative to handle the keys myself, instead of having one of my workers do it. I was leaving my spot when I was pulled over by the police. When they searched the car, they didn't even have a warrant, but they said their reason for pulling me over was because I made an illegal turn. Unfortunately for me, I had a gun on me that day, so when they searched the car, they found it.

I tried to beat it on the grounds of an illegal search, but my attorneys didn't win the case, and I ended up with a felony charge. With that first charge, I was put on probation, but then, I got hit with a drug charge. The day I got hit with the drug charge, I was in Queens, and I was driving a rental car at the time. I'd just finished picking up some drugs. I put it in my trunk and pulled off. I'm not sure if someone told on me or if they were watching me, but all of a sudden, a cop car pulls up behind me. Once he puts his lights on, all I could think about was getting away. There was no way with the number of drugs I had on me that I was going to take a chance, so I ended up in a high-speed chase with the police. I slammed into other cars and even bounced off a couple of cars. My car spun around, and the cops ended up running into me, which is how I got caught. I maxed out between the gun charge and the drug charge, so they sentenced me to three years. I ended up doing my time in Sing Sing and Elmyra, which were the maximum security facilities. As the time of your sentence lessens, you end up going to facilities with medium level security, because you're on your way home.

All the years I was trying to break into entertainment, and I ended up living in my world of entertainment. Some of the stuff I've been through can be a whole book. The hustle life is entertainment in and of itself. Selling drugs and living the lifestyle that is associated with the mob, rap and gang affiliations has hints of entertainment woven throughout it. My whole motivation behind hustling was never just to feed myself. The motivation was to entertain me and entertain the idea of being in the limelight. I was going to the same private events that rappers and entertainers were going to. Regular nine to five workers didn't have access to what I could access. My lifestyle in the streets coincided with what the stars were doing; only they had a craft that they could share with the world. Doing time in jail and doing what I did was all to feed my fantasy and to get to the lifestyle I wanted quickly.

My crew had to be the biggest and toughest guys in the club, even when we were in the mix of celebrities. Security and promoters knew who we were and we were getting VIP access just like people who were running in celebrity circles. It became a competition, and I was always aware of everything that came with the lifestyle I wanted. In my mind, accumulating money was associated with being famous and having notoriety. I was doing all the stuff stars were doing, and girls knew us just like girls knew the stars. The only thing I was missing was having the entertainment business behind me as I do now.

Before I even had a record out, I was seen as the biggest star in my neighborhood. There was a certain magnetism that I possessed, and people noticed it from the minute they met me. The only difference now is that I have real businesses that are solid and growing. I wanted to keep my mind in the flow of entertainment before even knowing that I would be a fixture in the business. Once I got in, I wasn't able to make my stamp like the other writers who transitioned into being artists. The Dream and Ne-Yo were able to capitalize off of their writing and leave a mark as an artist, which is something I haven't been able to master. I was the guy who idolized music, and I wanted to be the guy whose music people could say they could dance to or make love to his music. I've always carried the fabric of music around with me, so people automatically pick up on that. I would come to learn, however, that no facet of life nor entertainment could've prepared me for the biggest show of my life.

Mass Incarceration - White People's Entertainment

When I knew I was facing three years, I had no idea how much of the entertainment business would continue to follow me. However, it was different. I quickly became a controlled entertainer. I would now be told what to do,

NIKKO LONDON

how to do it and when to do it and time constraint became the new bully. I felt like I was an entertainer for the white guards and even some of my fellow prisoners. I remember one of my first confrontations with some other guys on my block and the correctional officers letting it happen. They would see stuff going on and just watch. It wasn't until they were done seeing enough that they made us go back to our cells.

I was already serving time in prison, and I was being punished on the inside. We had to buy their commissary, their food, and their products. When you are institutionalized, you end up being a puppet, and they get to laugh at you coming into their territory. They were always on our asses, even when we were doing what we were supposed to be doing. If you dropped something on the floor, you were yelled at and told to pick it up even when you were already bending down to pick it up. The inside is ten times worse than the outside. At least in the streets, you can leave or go somewhere else, but in the penitentiary, you're stuck until your time is up.

Everything was new to me my first day going in and most of what happened, I didn't expect to happen. There were about fifteen guys all chained along a wall, completely naked. They had to make sure you didn't bring any contraband into the prison. They make you throw your pants in the corner; then they dig in your mouth with their hands, which are covered in plastic gloves. They make you spread your butt cheeks, and they check everywhere. Then, they make you go in and get your jail uniform from another room. My first thought was who am I going to have confrontations with and how am I going to get through these next three years. I couldn't get comfortable for at least the first two weeks. I couldn't even go to sleep my first week because I wasn't sure if I was going to wake up. I didn't know who I was going to be sleeping around, so I had to have time to adjust.

During the first year of my three-year sentence, I was in Elmyra. I remember traveling there on a bus in chains. The entertainment started the minute I got off the bus. The correctional officers told the other inmates and me to line up against the wall and spread our butt cheeks. Even when we would do what they asked us, they would pick on us by telling us to reach our hands higher. It's like taunting you even when you're doing what they told you to do. Everybody tells you when they are in prison that they didn't do what they are in for or that they got caught up in the mix of things. Some people were in there for twenty-five years for a kilo of cocaine. The system is designed to strip you and take everything from you, even stuff you may have had before you were imprisoned. The Rico Law affected so many black families during the late 80's. You could get caught with a kilo of pure cocaine powder, and you would do less time than you would get for a kilo of crack cocaine. It would be the same kilo, but you would get twenty-five years for crack cocaine.

Before getting to Elmyra, I was on Riker's Island for six months. In Riker's Island, I had a cellmate, and we were cool, but the challenge with having a cellmate is you don't know if you've bumped heads with someone in his crew or if you'll even get along well. I also didn't know why e was serving time. He had the bottom bunk, and I had the top. Because I always had that underlying fear of not waking up one day, I found myself up most nights. The cell is no bigger than a bathroom, and this guy could flip out at any given moment. The correctional officer's throw you in where they want, so they aren't concerned with whether or not the person you're in a cell with might kill you one night. All of it is about manipulation - how can we control these animals and appease our frustrations. Eventually, we started talking, and I realized how cool he was. I found out he had a murder charge, which confused me as to why we were in the same cell since our classifications didn't match. It was clear that someone was setting us up, either to get into a fight or for one of us to kill ourselves. It's a fear factor in jail, and after a while, it becomes a big game to the correctional officers because they get to go home and tell their families exciting stories about their day. Here you are fighting the inmates and the correctional officers every day, not because you want to, but because you want to survive.

There was a kid in there that was facing twenty-five to life. He was from Flatbush, and we ended up bumping heads. Whenever we were walking through the prison, we always had to walk in a line. We were going to the mess hall, and his unit was coming back from the mess hall. There ended up being a big brawl in the hallway, so he jumps off of the line and tries to get to me. He had a razor and tried to cut me in my face, but it didn't catch me. I ended up in the infirmary that day, which was one of my only times there. There was another guy that I had a run in with before. We already had tension between us and there was a memo that he and I needed to remain separated. They had purposely switched us knowing that. Somehow, he was coming back from court, and we ended up in the same cell. He looks at me, and we immediately exchange words. We start to wrestle and tussle on the floor, and I ended up cut in my face this time. Razors were a major problem in prison, and most guys found a way to get one. Many occasions, the correctional officers know who isn't getting along or who doesn't like the other. They might put you in a cell with someone they know that you've had problems with in the past. I knew then that my next three years weren't going to be easy at all.

My First Year

My first year in the state pen, I was in Sing Sing Correctional Facility, a maximum security prison, located about 30 miles north of New York City in the Village of Ossining, NY. There were more people from my neighborhood in there than I had expected. It's never fun being in jail, but when you see someone you know, it becomes more comfortable. It also helps you when it comes to people giving you respect. One day, I was going to the mess hall with my prison block, but we were in there with other prison blocks. A guy got up from his seat and pulled something out and stabbed another guy in the neck. It started a huge riot in the mess hall, and that's when I realized anything could happen in the jail system. When you see stuff like that, you start to wonder if the correctional officers are in on it. They can choose to break it up or not or allow it to go on until someone gets killed.

Being in a city jail like Riker's Island, which sits on the East River between Queens and the Bronx. It is one of the world's largest correctional institutions and mental institutions. Being in there is literally like being in your neighborhood, but going to a state pen is an entirely different experience. You have to get permission to do everything that you want, from going to the library to the bathroom. I had guys coming up to me saying that they got railroaded and didn't even do some of the things they were accused of doing. My experience with legal aids is that they make deals for you, but their purpose is to make deals, not to get you out. Having a legal aid is like getting guaranteed time, it just boils down to how much time you're going to get. The legal aid is free, and they make you think it's going to work for you, but he's being paid by the government. It's absurd to think that the legal aid will fight against the person whose paying him.

I would see guys going to the law library learning about their case, but it would take seven years just to gather all the necessary information and get a chance to appeal. You go up in front of the board with four white guys in the room, and they're ready to judge you from the rip. Legally, if you've had no infractions, you're supposed to go home, but they start looking at your body language, the tone of your voice and everything else about your demeanor. When I went to the board for my release, they let me go the first time. I had one minor infraction while I was in, which was for fighting. I got five days in the hole for that, but other than that I didn't have any other infractions or behavioral issues.

I had heard what the hole was like throughout the pen. Everybody told me how horrible it was, but I think they didn't explain it well enough. The first day I went in, I thought five days could be knocked out quickly. But you can't do anything including, read a book, talk to anyone or get a shower unless you ask. Even going to sleep is difficult because you're in there for twenty-four hours. The first day felt like five in and of itself. I remember talking to the walls and talking to myself. The second day is when things started to take effect. I couldn't get commissary, visits or anything while I was in the hole. I couldn't watch television or have any entertainment, not even a deck of cards. The only thing in there with me was a toilet.

It was a horrible experience that I wouldn't wish on my worst enemy. Being in the hole is like being in a jail inside of a prison. I was next to other boxes where guys were also in the hole, and they were used to it because some of them had been in for thirty days. They put your meals through a hole in the door, and you eat on a scheduled time. Some people would scratch themselves or hurt themselves just to get out the box for a few hours and go to the infirmary. There was a particular day that you could go to the infirmary and they would end up taking people all at once, and unless you were dying, they wouldn't take you until that day.

Going to the infirmary gave you a chance to get some fresh air because you get to walk through the halls and it took at least three hours just to be seen, so it was like a break from hell. By day three, I felt like I had been in for ten days. I was doing the same thing over and over and over again. I was screaming for the infirmary at this point, but the guards would tell me that I had to wait. I would talk to the guys who had already lost their minds in the hole next door to me, and I started feeling like I was losing my mind, too. I was building a relationship with the guys who were completely mental at this point. I couldn't shave, and I knew that I looked like some wild beast because I felt like one. There were days I wouldn't even take a shower because going to the shower was a tease and it wasn't a real break from the hole.

I started to act like a big baby, refusing food and showers. I started pouting and refusing to do the things that they asked me to do. If prison breaks you, solitary confinement, also called 'the hole,' breaks you inside and out. By the fourth day, it got a little easier because I knew that I would be getting out the next day, so I began to focus on that. It was better than being in there for months at a time like some of the other inmates. Before you come out of the hole, they shackle your hands and ankles. The hole takes an enormous mental toll on you, and the guards have no idea what they will be introduced to when you come out. When I was released, I had developed a different aggression, and I was angrier at society. Once you experience the hole, you have a whole different mindset that from the outside looking in, makes you look crazy. You're more ferocious, and you're ready for anyone that tries you. I'd seen a darkness that most inmates hadn't seen. It put me on a higher level, and I went back to my cell block feeling cocky. Some of the inmates were screaming my name liked I'd been missed, and something great just happened. They were asking me how things went and I felt like I was being worshiped. I ended being moved from by block to a different block, and the guy that I had fought ended up being transferred to another prison.

 I know everyone asks men when they are in prison if they experienced being raped or if they've turned gay. I was never tested in prison when it comes to being turned into a man's bitch. There are two type of guys in prison - Chihuahuas and pit bulls, and I was the latter. A lot of the men that end up coming out of prison gay had some feminine trait in them. It's usually detected the moment they walk through the door. I've never had that kind of experience because, from the moment I walked in, the other inmates could sense that I was a beast. The same aura I carried in the streets was the same aura I carried in prison. My days in prison taught me a lot when it came to how the prison system is set up as a large corporation that capitalizes off of the pain and misery of black families. I'm not saying that everyone in there is innocent, but there are a lot of innocent people in prison - a lot of innocent black people. I just knew that once I got out, I was never going back. I had to get back to what I was good at - entertainment.

LIES

CHAPTER 13
I Never Slept With...

I first met Nicole Murphy in 2007 down in Miami. I was living down there at this time. One night, I was out hanging out with some friends, cruising the streets. I see these two women driving, and we caught up with them and started flirting. Nicole was on vacation so we told them to follow us to the Versace Mansion and they agreed. We ended up going swimming and later that night, her and I hung out. When she was leaving, we decided to keep in touch, and we started to develop a friendship. I didn't see her again until I went out to LA in 2008 to do business and I called her up to see if she wanted to hang out. She told me to meet her at this restaurant out in Sherman Oaks, called Casa Vega. After that, whenever I would come out to LA, we always tried to link up. I would go back to New York, and I told her that I would give her a call when I got back out to LA. This was when Michael Strahan came into the picture. I was trying to get her to come out to New York, but things kept popping up.

Somehow, he went through her phone and started calling people. When she found out, she gave me a heads up. She told me that he might call. Because she gave me the heads up, I was able to maneuver the conversation with him once he did call. When my phone did ring, it was a call from a strange number, and of course, it's him. He said, "Who's this?" I wasn't giving him any information, so I pushed back and asked him the same thing. He claims that he was just calling to see who the number belonged to because it kept coming up on her phone, but he presented it like it was his phone. The conversation didn't last too long. I called her and let her know about the call. Once I saw the pictures and the news in the tabloids that she was engaged to him, I fell back from her. We were still cool, but I wanted to respect her situation.

 We hung out another time after that, around Grammy weekend. AJ Calloway had an event, and I invited her out. It seemed like whenever we would reconnect, we would lose touch again. Little did I know that Mimi would be the reason that we reconnected again in 2015. I got a call from Nicole Murphy one night, but it wasn't a call that I was expecting. She informed me that there was a rumor out there that she and I had a sex tape floating around. I didn't have time to be shocked by that because then she told me that Mimi was the one that called her and told her about it. Nicole and Mimi don't know each other and have never spoken before. Nicole wanted to know how Mimi had gotten her number. Mimi went out of her way to warn Nicole so that she could tell her to be careful. This was after she and I had released our sex tape.

It was a messy situation because Nicole and I had never slept together. I was trying to keep Nicole calm about the whole thing, especially since she was seeing Michael Strahan. I told her not to worry about it because we're both aware how crazy this industry is and how the rumors go. Later that night, Nicole and I hung out at Nick's, this place in Beverly Hills. We were having drinks and catching up with old friends. While we're hanging out, Mimi calls Nicole's phone again. Nicole goes to answer it, but then Mimi sends her a text. At that point, Nicole turns to me and says she wants nothing to do with it. All I could do was shake my head.

Somehow, TMZ found out that Nicole and I were hanging out at Nick's. Nicole's friend, who was also at Nick's with a few other friends, came over to us and told us that they were out there. When we were about to leave, her girlfriend told us that we couldn't leave out the front knowing how messy the situation could get between Nicole and Michael. It was bad enough that she had Mimi calling her about a sex tape. I left alone and got twenty-one questions from TMZ about Nicole, but I held my ground that we were just friends. To this day, I have no idea who started the sex tape rumor, but I was just glad that it didn't affect her relationship.

NIKKO LONDON

Selita Ebanks

I met Selita at a function in Manhattan back in 2002. We became friends and started hanging out. I would pick her up from her place in Upper West Side Manhattan, and we would just drive around Manhattan. She would tell me about her modeling career and how she was trying to reach certain goals. This was another beautiful woman that had entered my space, but we never slept together. I always respected her as a friend. Our communication fizzled out as she started to make moves in her industry and I was making moves in mine.

One thing I remember so vividly about her was that she spoke her dreams into existence. Ten years before becoming a Victoria's Secret model, she would always tell me that she was shooting a modeling campaign in LA and she was going to make it big. She believed in herself so much that she always spoke about how successful was going to become. She said it on a regular basis - that she was going to be Victoria's Secret model. Even though I didn't believe her, something about the conviction in which she said it made me realize it might be possible.

Here it is, after all these years of conversations where she was saying it and preparing for it, she's now walking in her dreams. She's heavily involved in what she dreamed for herself. She spoke high about it before she even seen it come to life. I can honestly say I'm proud to know her, but not because she's famous, but because she gave was giving me hope at that moment, and neither of us realized it. I mentioned these two women to set the

SEX, ENTERTAINMENT & LIES

record straight on anything that may be floating around about us. I give respect where it's due, and I have slept with enough women that I have no reason to lie.

CHAPTER 14
Sex Tape Addressed

The sex tape fiasco wasn't as complicated as everyone tried to make it seem. Mimi and I had sex every night as a couple, so we decided to do something that was edgy. The filming came into play one night when we were at her house. I brought up the idea of us filming, but it was a mutual conversation, and we were both cool with it. There was never a second where a video camera was set up, and she didn't know. We ended up filming ourselves having sex about three or four times. We never looked at them right away, but the purpose was to look back at them and eventually have sex to our tape. There was only one copy of the tape with several sessions on it.

What triggered us to put our sex tape out and connect with a big company was a conversation we'd had around the end of the third season of *Love & Hip Hop*. It was all premeditated, and there weren't any surprises. Things were shaky for both of us as far as the show, and we weren't sure if they were going to ask us to come back. Things were also bad between her and Stevie and at this point, she wanted to get back at him. She told me he was saying a lot of disrespectful and nasty things to her and she would leave his presence feeling broken. From the minute we talked about it, we were always thinking how we could trump whatever Stevie and Joseline had going on. We also thought about the notoriety we were going to get from this moment. We knew it would be big, but we weren't prepared for the outcome of how big it was.

We knew we would be the talk of the town putting our sex tape out. For both of us, it was a trump card - for her to get back at Stevie and for me to make some money. We talked about all the affects that it would have later on her daughter and possibly even her career if we did this deal with Vivid Entertainment. We had several talks in between, and there was never a moment that we were caught off guard. The tape got the reaction we wanted. The only thing that we were caught off guard with was the timing. We didn't even know that it was going to shock the industry, but we did know it would definitely secure a spot for us on the next season of *Love & Hip Hop*.

As far as the negotiation went for the tape, I negotiated it so that the percentage would work for both of us for the rest of our lives. We made a decision to jump out this boat together. Before we did the deal with Vivid Entertainment, we were in the Bahamas. She had been on the show longer than me, so she knew how to work the producers. She asked me how we were going to say the tapes got leaked. I was willing to take the hit, and since we were traveling, I was the one that said I would say that I lost it in my bag. She agreed to it because she knew this would work for her being on *Love & Hip Hop* another season. At that time, we thought we had to come up with a story because it would give us a stronger story line.

To stretch it out with episodes, we had to come up with a way to draw out the storyline. This was like an easy layout for the show, and we had already come up with a plan, so the show decided to make it seem like I leaked the tape. Even when I wasn't in a scene with Mimi, my name was being dropped by that point. I never stopped to think whether or not my mother would see it, but compared to the past I already had, the tape was minute to me. Unfortunately, a lot of our youth worship that, especially because of the music business. Sex is glorified in the rap game and in the world of entertainment that I live in, having a sex tape is acceptable.

The way the whole deal worked with Vivid Entertainment proves that I wasn't the mastermind of anything. Vivid had seen the home video that we made, but that's not how they operate when it comes to putting out a tape. They need professional, high-quality shots that they can show their audience, and our home video wasn't enough. We were nervous at first because we aren't porn stars, but we had already signed the contract. They flew us back out to where they are in LA, and they got us a hotel room. It was weird for us because what we had created was fun and relaxing, but now, we're in front of another person, which was a woman, filming us, and we had to have sex in front of her. We were drinking and trying to get into it, but it wasn't working. The next day, we tried it again, and we had no choice but to do it because they couldn't extend our stay any longer.

Mimi didn't want to do it, but I explained to her that we had to commit to it because we had already signed a contract. I think it was just uncomfortable for both of us because we were in front of someone. We start going at it again, and I couldn't even get it up. I told Mimi I needed to pull the camera lady in the mix and I knew I would be able to get hard again. I asked Mimi if it was okay, even though I wasn't even sure the woman with the camera was going to go with it. I went over to her and started talking, and I told her the only way this would work is if she participated with us. All she did was get naked, and I was able to play with her vagina and get back in the groove. By now, I'm back up, and everybody seems to be more comfortable.

Once I started having sex with Mimi, we got right into it and moved from the bedroom to the living room. That's when the lady suggested that we go into the bathroom. I didn't want to do it bending Mimi over the sink or anything that was normal, so we got in the shower and turned on the water. That's when she grabbed the shower rod, and we went in heavy. That day, we were able to film for three hours. It was very challenging trying to film for production - you have to get relaxed for each scene, somebody is watching you the whole time, and you have to stop so they can get the right angles.

Surprisingly, the woman stayed naked the whole time so we could get the scene done.

I would do another sex tape with my woman, but I wouldn't exploit myself again. Mimi and I were together, but we were more "together" when it came to business. I'm not the kind of man that wants my woman out there, but we were having fun with it, and we were doing business together, and it worked for us. We had a sexual chemistry for each other. My view of our relationship was different than it would be with someone that I see longevity with as a couple. I would've never done anything like this with Margeaux because she wouldn't have gone for it.

The downside to having a sex tape out there for the world to see is not having the control to spin it the way you want when it comes out. The way people came at me and judged me was also a downside. I didn't go hard when it came to defending myself and when it came to responding to a lot of the blogs. There were a lot of people that were telling me that I had to put something out as far as a statement, but I didn't. Now that the tape has been out for a while, I honestly don't see many downsides to it. The thing that changed the excitement of the video for me was that I was now in it alone. There were a lot of people in Mimi's ear, so it was as she threw me under the bus to make herself look good. I was okay with that because I can hold my own. I just wanted the truth to be out there that I never dogged this woman and I didn't try to exploit her.

SEX, ENTERTAINMENT & LIES

Gay Rumors

I only feel the need to address the gay rumors because they were the ones that affected my business the most. When Johnny and I were shooting the video for the song NY to LA, we were at the airport with the private jet behind us having a good time. I asked Mimi to be in the video, and I was aware that there were going to be other guests on the set. I had even invited a few people on set. The show had discussed other people being on the set with me, but they never talked about the monkey wrench that they were throwing in. That's what got me most upset about the scene with K. Michelle. They came to me and said they wanted to shoot me shooting the video. It was a day that I couldn't originally film for *Love & Hip Hop* because I had the video shoot locked in and we had already paid for space. For them, that was a good thing, and they wanted to include it as a scene.

That was a big deal to Johnny and me. We were all getting ready and preparing for the video when K. Michelle came onto the set and started creating friction. I think they wanted her to have conflict with me, but the show knew upsetting Mimi wasn't a good idea. She was already distraught and going through it with Stevie, so they used K. Michelle to ruffle my feathers for that scene. Unfortunately, the gay rumor affected the tone of who I was. It wasn't about a brand because at the time I was just a behind the scenes regular guy from Brooklyn. However, promoters stopped bringing me out to do walkthroughs, and it was hard to make money in the marketplace because people started questioning me. The business side of what I was doing was starting to get messed up because there was a persona around my name that came from that scene and people read into the persona.

My mother talked me through a lot of it and encouraged me to push past the rumors. She was a huge impact when it came to me bouncing back from the gay rumors. The real thing that kept me going was that I got to know who I was at that time. I had to start looking at things from a different angle. I was in a space where I felt lost in my world. It wasn't that I was down and out about any fall out I received from the show. I got down on myself because I felt like had lost control. I knew what I signed up for, even if I didn't know how it was all going to go. It wasn't about me pointing fingers or blaming someone for what happened, even with the rumors putting a negative light on my image. I just couldn't believe that I had lost so much control.

Gay Sex Tape Rumor

Before this, I had never even heard my name associated with another sex tape. Around the time Mimi started acting funny with the sex tape, Stevie and I had an argument on the show. His way of trying to get back at me was threatening to release some bogus sex tape. He claimed I was having sex with a male model, but that was a flat out lie. He said if I moved forward with the sex tape with Mimi, he would release the tape. MediaTakeOut got a hold of the story, and it went viral, but obviously it was all a lie. If it wasn't; why didn't he release this so-called tape? You know why; because the tape doesn't exist. I've never been with a man and for Stevie to say that and not even come through with the tape made no sense. My biggest frustration with people is why the gay rumor always comes up when somebody doesn't like you. Stevie started that rumor quite during my last season on the show.

If it was true, wouldn't a gay guy have come forward by now and said something? Here I was, the most hated man on reality television and some people hate me, yet if this tape existed, why didn't it surface by now? Joseline even threw out there that I was gay because I didn't have children. It's like the ammunition people use to sabotage you when they start hating you. Stevie's biggest challenge with me was that I was in his league and I had been with Mimi. I was on the show, and we were in competition, so he had to try and find something on me to try and knock me down.

I spoke with Fred, the owner of MediaTakeOut.com and he informed me that he had to put the story out. He asked me if it was true and was there a tape out there. Even though I said no, I didn't even tell him not to put the story up. I told him it was a lie, but I understood he was going to run the story anyway because that's the way the blogs work. I knew that Stevie didn't have anything to show for what he said, so I dropped it. If I would've told him not to run the story, I would look guilty, so my hands were pretty much tied.

NIKKO LONDON

Love & Hip Hop was a money moment for me. It wasn't like I was in acting school for six months, I did a major film and then came over to reality television. I guess because some people think that reality television is a career, it seems like that's all you have. Of course, I wanted to capitalize on the moment, so I had a publicist that wanted to do some pro-bono work for me. I wanted to see what he could do for my career, so I agreed. He set me up to do an interview with the Hot Topic Radio Show in Vegas, but I didn't go. The host of the show talked trash about me for a whole hour, and I wasn't even there. It was supposed to be a call-in radio interview, and I wasn't feeling the idea of just walking into an interview without knowing what was going on. The publicist had set it up and just threw it at me.

I asked him to give me a few times that I would be able to do the interview, especially since it was live session. I didn't quite understand why he felt he needed to help me rebuild my brand, especially since most of what people knew about me had nothing to do with my brand. I wasn't sure what he was trying to do, so I decided not to call in to do the interview. Even my music business partner Johnny Chrome, who did the video NY to LA with me, turned on me and filmed a scene with Mimi saying that he was the mastermind behind me being on the show. He also told her that I was looking to film her and expose her via the sex tape, which was all a lie. He told people he was just on the show to get his music out and that he had come to Atlanta to get his music career going.

Things didn't pan out the way he planned, especially when I started to film with *Love & Hip Hop*. That became my primary focus, and the music took a backseat. I think he thought because we were friends that he would be able to be on the show with me. The more scenes I started to do with Mimi, the more envious he became. They only called him for the one scene with K. Michelle and the one with Mimi. I guess at some point because they hadn't reached back out to him, he started to feel like I played him. I had to wait to be called for the show, so I wasn't sure what kind of pull he thought I had.

I sat around for two whole months waiting for them to call me, yet he was expecting for me to be able to pull strings to get him on. Even my mom was upset because she knows Johnny and he was like a son to her, but again, Mona and the producers had to get what they needed by any means necessary. Because he switched up on me, they looked at it like there must be some truth to everything that he was saying. He was cool with both my wife and me. Even Maarguex said she couldn't believe he lied. Margeaux and I would try to fix things like this, but it was always too late. It felt like when we saw the episodes or the blog posts; we had so much catching up to do that it wasn't even worth it.

It's almost like whoever tells their truth first is the one people will believe. The problem with that is the person speaking first isn't always telling the truth, or they tell it and spin, so it makes them look like a victim. I don't think I'd ever experienced it to such a high degree until Margeaux and I were sued by Supa Fly Entertainment.

CHAPTER 15
Lawsuits and Lies

When I first met Tim Dawg, it was back in 1998. At the time, he was the Vice President of Epic Records, and he was the one that signed me to a deal with them. Norman Bordeur had a company called Supa Fly Entertainment, and I had a company called IMMusic Group. I had Margeaux signed to IMMusic Group, and we did a deal with Supa Fly Entertainment that started with the song *SuperFine*. Tim Dawg was the guy who connected me to Supa Fly, and Norman Bordeur was the investor that we partnered with. Somehow, Tim Dawg ended up being the A&R for both companies, which was a conflict of interest. He was working with us but getting paid from them, but it was working. We were friends, so we proceeded.

This was also around the time that I was working with Timbaland, Jim Beanz and another producer named, Major Hands. I told them about Norman Bordeur and the opportunity I had, which is how things started to connect again in music, but something began to feel strange. Norman had begun doing things that made me uncomfortable. He started dressing like me and trying to mimic my lifestyle, and I started to realize that he was trying to get in the business off of my relationships and that he wasn't trying to be a record executive - he was trying to be an entertainer.

His mistress at the time filled me in on how much he admired me and was always trying to mimic my style. I didn't let it bother me until he started trying to take over my company. We were doing a partnership, and he was trying to tell me how much money to spend on my record. When I went to Tim with it, he started telling me to let Norman do what he thought was best because Norman knew what he was doing. I didn't understand why Tim was on his side because we were friends. He wasn't even trying to see things from our point of view because this guy was paying him. I later found out that Norman was also in Tim's ear when we weren't around. It didn't make sense to me that Tim was telling me to listen to Norman when it came to setting prices for relationships I already had in place. So, I told Tim that I needed to be in the loop from that moment forward.

I tried to explain to Norman that if he went to Timbaland and the other producers, they were going to charge him one price, but when I go to them, they were going to charge me a lower price because I had the relationships. The only way Norman could control me was through Tim Dawg, the same way *Love & Hip Hop* could only control me through Mimi, so Norman started telling Tim that he wanted Margeaux and not me. He saw her as the star and the one with the potential. Tim came to me and told me that Norman wanted Margeaux, but I said no. That's when Tim started bringing up the contract and telling me I had to uphold my end. I knew that something was shaky because Tim was telling me I had to adjust but not telling Norman to do the same.

Norman no longer had our best interest at heart and Tim was giving me the same vibe, so I decided to get my manager and lawyer. Tim Maddenbomb was the lawyer that we hired, and he linked us with Tony Draper, who at the time was with Swab House Records out of Houston. Now, Margeaux and I had a new team to go up against Supa Fly Entertainment. That's when all hell broke loose. Norman had somehow worked out a deal for us at Universal Records, but he decided to go up there without the group because he thought he could do the deal without us. Monte Lipman, the president of Universal Records at the time, was interested in signing us. He genuinely wanted to work with us. Norman had gone to Universal with contracts showing that we were signed to him. Too bad he wasn't smart enough to figure out his conniving plan before he went up there because the executives knew something was off with Norman based off of his conversation.

Once he realized that he couldn't do anything without us, that's when he got Tim to call us. Tim called us the next day and told us that Universal wanted to meet with us, but the way Tim explained it was as if this would be their first encounter with our brand when in reality it wasn't. Once we were done talking to Tim, our lawyer stepped in, and that's when we got the manager. When we all arrived at Universal, they sat us down and told us about the original meeting. Tony called me and said "I like the music I heard and I can come in and fix this. Just put me in contact with Norman."

I put him in contact with Norman, but unfortunately, Norman got upset while they were talking. Tony was trying to fix it so that things could end smoothly and everything could continue because there was a million dollar deal on the table. Tony couldn't get through to Norman even though he made it so that Norman would still walk away with everything that was originally promised, but Norman got greedy and wouldn't agree. We ended up going back to Universal, and they offered us the deal. Universal said that they would continue working on the situation with Norman and give him what he wanted so we could seal the deal officially. By now, Tim Maddenbomb becomes partners with us.

Norman called the President of Universal the next day and asked him, "Am I able to do this deal and be a part of it all the way without having just to take certain points?" Universal was going to give him his fair share and take control of the group from there. They were going to give him everything that was in the contract, but he would have no access to them or us, which wasn't what Norman wanted. The president was pissed off at this point, and now, Monte is no longer interested. He felt like it was causing too many problems and we hadn't signed with them yet. This was four days before Christmas of 2007. I couldn't believe the chance for us to be millionaires was right at the tip of our fingers and a bad connection ruined everything.

Now, Norman is upset and accusing us of messing up the deal, so he ends up sending our lawyer, Tim, letters threatening to sue us. He sent about three different letters. He also sent Margeaux letters threatening to have her deported, which was the reason we rushed and got married in 2008. Our lawyer and manager started working to see how we could get out of everything with Norman. Since Tim Dawg was our manager before we went and got Tony, hiring Tony made Tim feel like we were pushing him out. This led to us falling out. I didn't concern myself with the way he felt because I already felt like he had sold Margeaux and I out when he had chosen Norman's side over ours.

The lawsuit was bogus, but we didn't have money to fight the way we needed to. Our lawyer told us the lawsuit wouldn't go very far and that's why it's still pending. People sue all the time in this business, but it doesn't mean they are going to win. Norman and I never talked again after that, and it also scarred my friendship with Tim Dawg. He was getting money from Norman under the table the whole time. Him and didn't talk for over six years. It wasn't until *Love & Hip Hop* that we reconnected and I was the one who initiated contact. When we started talking again, we just brushed the whole Norman situation under the rug. Tony Draper and the lawyer were trying to help us, but we were all burned out at this point. Nobody wanted to touch us with this lawsuit hanging over our heads. Once again, my music career lingered in the nosebleed seats while I had to sit back and watch everyone else perform at halftime.

CHAPTER 16
Love & Hip Hop Didn't Give Me Identity

If I had to describe who I was before *Love & Hip Hop*, I would say I was a Ghetto Superstar. I grew up in the city of dreams, where creating your reality was possible every day. I was born and raised in Brooklyn, but I've lived in the Bronx, Queens, and Manhattan. I was very well known throughout New York. I was the kid who always hustled and knew how to get to the next move. How could *Love & Hip Hop* define a kid from Brooklyn who had the world in the palm of his hands before he even understood what that meant? I was always the kid looking for another step on the ladder and wondering how to get things done.

If there didn't seem to be a way to get it done, I found one. People in my neighborhood saw me as a cool, down to earth kid. I was a little rough around the edges, but I always an enigma, and it often left people wondering, which was good because I never wanted to be easy to figure out. I was raised in one of the toughest cities in America, so being able to move and shake without everyone figuring you out was the key to survival. At some point, I became the fly guy that had a bunch of cars and could move and shake with the best of them. I could mingle and hang with anyone, whether Blacks, Asians, Russians or Italians.

I knew who I was, where I was from and I represented myself well. But I was always intrigued by other races and things outside of my culture. This helped me in a lot of ways because New York is a huge melting pot. You can either learn how to maneuver through it, or you can get lost in it. I chose to maneuver and created my blueprint. My biggest goal was always to look for the better way, strive for something new and reach for better things. I wasn't different from many of the kids on the block; I just thought differently. I never allowed society to dictate to me how I should be or how I should grow.

A lot of people allow society to do that and most of them don't even realize it's happening. If someone gave me a book and said "you should do this or do that," I researched it. You can't hand Nikko a book and tell him to do something. I have to figure out how to do it my way and make it work to my advantage, no matter how positive or good it is. I wasn't just going to do anything just because someone said it would be good for me. What's good for you may be bad for me and vice versa. Having my flow put me in a position to win early in life. While most people were figuring it out via education or through others, I was creating my educational program.

Essentially, this caused me to be an outcast. I was even the outcast in my family because I always went a different way out and I never stuck to the norm. I just couldn't accept mediocrity, and I didn't see myself getting lost in the streets or the system. I had my moments, and I've definitely lived the street life, but again, I always saw a better way. There's no way a show like *Love & Hip Hop* could give a kid like me from Brooklyn his identity. But, I was put in a box after my first season on the show, and I could feel it right away. How did the Ghetto Superstar end up being on a show where he couldn't at least be himself? I knew what I was doing it for, but I can honestly say I was lost. I got lost for two minutes on a journey that I thought I was in control of, that ended up having control over me. As someone whose served time in prison, this was the first time since doing my three year bid that I felt like someone else had control over me.

I've worked a few nine-to-fives in my life, and I hated it. I did it because I had to and I do whatever I need to make my next move a guaranteed move. A nine-to-five always made me feel stuck like I couldn't do what I needed when I needed and working on *Love & Hip Hop* was like working a nine-to-five all over again. It was a gift and a curse, and I would've handled it a lot differently had I known exactly what I was getting myself into. There's this notion that people in reality television should already know what they are getting into because the formula is pretty much the same on every network.

I have to clear that up. Contracts are written, and they tell you what it's going to be, so I would never say you don't know, but with all the editing that's done, more goes on and more gets taped than people see. We aren't just snapping on each other and causing problems just because we want to. Before you saw that fist fly, there were at least three hours of footage, and most of it was a build-up. There are some things you don't sign up for when you sign that contract. You don't know what's going to happen on a day-to-day basis with these shows, but once you sign the dotted line, the whole scene can change and it, just like the contract, will always be in the networks favor.

I was confined to their timeline, their edits and their structure. I was portrayed like a nobody that needed the show to make him a somebody. The whole aura that people got was that I was a leech that was trying to live off of Mimi. So the end goal didn't pan out the way I wanted because I came there to get notoriety for the music and in some ways, I lost focus and got complacent. I take full responsibility for that because I did three seasons and at some point, I could've stopped it. I didn't even get paid for the first season. The first season was my way of establishing myself on the show, but after the first season, there was income. It was something to hold on to, and I could've let it go after the second season. Everybody that's on reality television knows the moment they sign that contract that you are denouncing your rights, your identity, your values and your persona. They get to put your image out there as the way they want to perceive you and the way they want people to see you. You are a character, and you have to play it well because if you don't, you're done. If you don't play the character well, they will make one for you or they will cut you off. I didn't play the villain character the way they wanted me to, but I was needed for Mimi. I was the necessary evil, so even if they wanted to cut me, they couldn't.

If people want to judge me for what they saw on the show; I get it. I may have had my moments of wandering, but I didn't sell out, and I stayed true to myself; even if I was portrayed differently. *Love & Hip Hop* didn't allow me to tell my story the way I would have. I didn't have the proper platform because on a show like that, humanity is lost and you're judged from the gate. I get telling a great story and giving it life, but my truth would've given the show more life than it did with all the lies. Making it one sided doesn't allow both parties involved to be portrayed correctly. I was portrayed as a sneaky, shady guy with no morals, but I still did my job. I didn't give them any hassle or play games with the show, but yet, I was seen as a horrible person who didn't care about a woman I loved.

Even after all this, I would do *Love & Hip Hop* again. I would just make sure it's done differently. I'm thankful and grateful for the platform and the opportunity I had to put myself out there. I was just caught off guard and had to figure it out as we moved along. I think the thing that hurts the most is how black people react to and treat each other when it comes to stuff like this. It hurts me when my people ride the negative train for so long. As black people, we set trends, and we have a culture that the rest of the world follows. We have so much influence, and we don't always recognize that. We're so slave minded that we don't know how to keep the value in our community. No other race treats each other the way we do, and this continues to push us backward.

The producers are in it for the business, that's their job. But we could've found a way as the cast to make wise moves when it came to the business as well. Unfortunately, we don't understand economics as it pertains to bartering. What would have happened if we'd all come together and saw it from the angle of how important we were to the show and that even with our differences, we can work together? Even if we don't like each other, how can we build off this and make it work for all of us? Unfortunately, nobody thought like that. I was thinking about the business, but I was the low man on the totem pole.

Instead of looking at it as a unit driven opportunity, we divide and tear each other down, and it messes up the business side of things. If we understood keeping the money circulated in the black community, our opportunities would be different. Most people reading this won't even realize that our dollars stay in the black community for only six hours. The Jewish community keeps theirs in for about six days, and in China, it stays there for about eleven days. What does that say about how divided we are? You have a reality television show on a network that's completely about the business, and this is what you see, black people divided and hating on each other instead of looking to win together. We don't get the economic system of jumping on these shows and learning how we can make things happen for all of us.

We should all know how to play the game. This way, relationships are built, and the audience sees something different, but it's hard when you are dealing with talent who believes their stuff is better than the next person. I'm sure that when people read this, they'll be surprised. They see this dumb person who allegedly doesn't know how to keep his private matters together, who stepped in and swiped another man's woman with no respect. There needs to be some balance in reality television. Why do they think they can't have drama with balance? I think to portray black men on reality shows like they all are sleeping with thirty women, calling each other niggas and cursing every other word is absurd because not everyone has that truth. If you're going to have the negative guy, then have the guy on there that's a great father to his children as well. There should be a balance when it comes to portraying black men on television. Put them on there and let them be transparent on their own, not forced transparency with added story lines. Reality doesn't mean showing one side of a story and embellishing.

What *Love & Hip Hop* did do for me is give me more of a platform and an opportunity to be in front of people. The gift to that is I'm able to be me, but with a larger reach because I'm exposed to the world now more than ever. The problem is, it gave me a questionable identity to people who don't know my real identity. There's still a huge question mark after my name. People have either already decided who I am or they aren't sure what I stand for. That's the bad part, but with anything, you take the good with the bad, and you find a way to capitalize off of that. Even with this book, people will find a way to say "He's doing this for the money." Why wouldn't I find a way to capitalize off of the position I'm in? That's the Ghetto Superstar trait that's innate, and it's always going to be there.

People can be so jaded by entertainment, especially reality. You get to identify with a character with scripted dramas. When people see it, they find the people relatable. They can see why the character does what they do. But with reality, there's no thin line - people feel like they know you and they start to immediately take you seriously simply because of the word "reality." Is this who this guy *really* is? He can't be serious? This is why it's so important for me to continue to develop who I am and to pursue my calling, which I believe is to be a philanthropist and to help people improve their health and fitness. I want to be connected to people that want to see a change in their community. My goal as a philanthropist is to help ten people at a time change their lives, especially as it pertains to financial gain. It's important to get to a place where scarcity isn't an issue, so I want to help the people that are looking to be entrepreneurs.

What a lot of people don't get today is how to strategize to bring their ideas together. Ideas can be bought, but action steps and how you get there is what a lot of people need. I'm on a billion-dollar mission, so my focus and my fight are different. I want to help those people who can see themselves going where I'm going or who can at least see the vision clearly of where they're going. As far as my music, that is something that I will always do. I flow with the way I feel when I'm recording music. I'm not one for doing a lot of songs on pain and love because I like to focus on the feel good music. I'm free-spirited, so my music reflects that. That's not to say that music like that doesn't help me or get my creative juices flowing, but what I put out into the earth as far as my art reflects on me. I want people to feel great and excited listening to my music, not sad and depressed.

My biggest influences growing up were my parents. I saw both of my parents mature and grow before my eyes and that gave me the confidence I needed to grow up and do my own thing. I thought about what my parents went through whenever I came up against some rough issues, especially the pressures on national television and the moments of doubt. Because my parents were tough and they instilled that in me, I know I can handle anything. They showed me how to get around and how to launch back when life handed me a setback. The surprising thing was I know I didn't let my family down. They were proud of me and if anything, I think they saw it as a gain.

They knew I was determined to come up by any means necessary while staying true to myself. Even with people whispering about me and taking rumors back to my family, my mother always said to me "how are you going to turn this around?". Of course, there was some heavy concern. It was new, and anything new scares people. My mother could tell from our phone conversations, based on my tone how I was feeling. That's how she was able to gauge my emotions. She's my mother, and she wanted to make sure I was okay, but she reminded me of who I was.

I was intuitive to what was going on, but I was always thinking ahead. I wasn't reacting like most people wanted me to on the show, mainly because I understand who I am and what I have to offer. The way that I had learned how to master the streets and not be a statistic made me handle the show differently. I've always maintained my cool head, even when I had a moment of frustration on the show. I always called my shots, even though the show made it hard to do so most of the time. I was the one who left the show. I told them I'm moving to LA and I wasn't interested in signing the contract that they handed me. When they called me and asked me about doing *Love & Hip Hop: Hollywood*, I didn't feel like there was any honor there and they weren't even willing to raise my pay. They had a "take it or leave it" mentality, and I've never been in that situation before. I wasn't about to allow anyone to put me in that kind of situation now.

The perception of being super rich as a reality star is false. That's not to say that people are broke, but most people that come on these shows were in a situation where their money was a little shaky. So the illusion that there's a lot of money falling out of our pockets is just that - an illusion. As a hustler, there were times I did have $100,000 and was able to make that in four months, and there were times that I had a few bucks to get me by day-by-day. Reality television brings notoriety and can add to something that you're already doing like, music, fashion or modeling. I've made millions before, but I would never lie and say I came on the show with a lot of money. I came on with the understanding that I was going to make some money.

My objective now is to learn how to keep the money coming in. I could always make it, even though I had to take a couple of losses. I've never been in a consistent position where there was a constant flow of checks coming in. When I worked a nine-to-five, there was a weekly check, but for most of my life, there wasn't. The year and a half I took off from the club scene in LA were spent building my brand. At that moment I decided not to go back on *Love & Hip Hop*, and I had to figure out a way to earn an income. The break allowed me to start putting some things together and I had enough money to last me at least a year.

So I started training and hanging out with great people. When I was in Atlanta, I had one fitness model called the 4-Minute Fit. While in LA, I started coming up with ideas on how to expand that brand. I wanted the 4-Minute Fit idea to compete with the likes of Nike, so I started researching the fitness industry. I took the time to get into the inner workings of health and fitness. My company, Zeek Pak, started to take on a new shape. Since my interest goes from protein shakes to workouts and creating custom plans, I came up with the 24-Minute Challenge.

I found some people that could be apart of the beta system I created and trained them for free. It was about taking the new model and showing them how I can do it in twenty-four days. Then, I started thinking; I need to develop the music side. Even with all the music out on the internet, I always put out new music. I got caught up in the television thing and the thing that made me tick started to slip. I had to get back to the music. People were asking me for my music, telling me that it was inspiring them. The new single I have coming out is called 'No Hold Back,' which is being released on an independent label called, Unstoppable Music Group. I want to continue to grow my independent circuit before taking any deal that may be presented. Building the music aspect of my brand this time around will take more time because I want to make sure everything is solidified and strong before going to a label.

I'm also putting together a podcast. The podcast I'm doing talks about different topics as it pertains to health and wellness. It's an all around a model that touches on the mind, body, and soul. Zeek Pak is the umbrella, and everything else will flow from there. As I continue to develop my brand, everything that I put out will always go back to helping people win big in life. I'm essentially building something major, and this book is the last piece to the puzzle being complete. It's a chess move, and I know that it's going to solidify the brand and heighten the flow of everything else I'm doing.

The whole thing goes back to what I said in the beginning - this is my document, and this is going to be around as long as all the negative stories that are circulating. When people look me up, they'll see Zeek Pak Fitness, my teachings, and my book. They'll see the diversity of who I am and how I want my legacy to be shaped. It's important for me to show that a black man can build an empire and help others the same way other races do without having to look crazy on television. It's about depositing back into my people and my community even with all the negativity that surrounds my name. Because doing that is all about walking in my calling, the reason I'm here. That's the one thing that people can't take away from me - my calling.

Putting It All Into Perspective

The older I grew and the more I learned about my parents' marriage, the less I looked at marriage as merely a union of love. The years of perspective from my parents' marriage and my own had brought about the understanding that love, while important is a tool of marriage and not solely the foundation. I now look at marriage as a business and union meant to produce. Even as they are united, each has to bring their identity to the marriage. Marriages are built upon a bond of trust, love, friendship and sharing the same perspectives as you move toward building a family and business. Both adults are now responsible for each other, but they also have to be responsible for themselves. Decisions that are made are made as a union, not just individually. Whenever I decide to marry again, I will see it as a business regarding working together to build for the future, but I will be sure to see the other aspects of marriage as well.

With my current marriage to Margeaux, we both became too caught up in business, and as a result, we ended up freezing our emotions. Later in the relationship, we became so focused on business that our sex life was all but non-existent. The lack of sex soon became so toxic that it started to be a turnoff. We didn't take the time to secure the relationship like we should have, but on the other hand, we stayed focused on the hustle and were climbing the business ladder. We thought more about the career and the business than the relationship. The point soon came when the downward spiral of our relationship began to affect our business. Ultimately we essentially ended up putting a strain on both our relationship and business. With the foundation of our marriage not as strong as it should have been we weren't prepared to work together as business partners. We couldn't separate the two aspects of our relationship, so when problems arose in our marriage, they transferred over making it difficult to fix any business issues we were having. I know that age doesn't always guarantee wisdom, but I can't help but think that since I am ten years older than Margeaux that maybe I should've been able to avoid many of our missteps and handled it all differently. Although we were long separated maybe I would have gone on *Love & Hip Hop: Atlanta* and maybe I wouldn't have, but at the time I had my reasons.

In and of itself being featured on a television show can be a gift and a curse, even more so when you're married. It can be a gift to a marriage when you know that the two of you aren't getting along at the moment. Television may offer the opportunity for you to address your issues while providing financial gain. The downside is that along with the opportunity comes having to expose your life and your marriage, but if the marriage is already on the outs, there seems to be nothing to lose especially if you're both up front with each other. One or maybe even both of you may have loose ends to tie up, such as a new significant other, before appearing on television so as not to surprise the other. It sounds crazy, but if you both go into it with the mindset of keeping everything on a business level, you can get along just to get the filming done.

Looking back on it, all I can honestly say is one of the main reasons why Margeaux and I are still together is for business. Ironically, for better or for worse the one thing we've always valued in each other is how we conduct business. I don't know the statistics behind it all, but I'm sure that our approach to our marriage and television is not that uncommon in entertainment. In fact, I know so. Recently one-half of a wildly popular television couple stated in an interview that although they had shared eleven seasons together, she had been thinking about divorce since right before their show began. She went on to share that they weren't happy in their relationship and how although they were married, they weren't together in any other sense. I identified with the interview more than anyone could ever imagine and found myself once again in a similar state when Margeaux and I later appeared on WE Television's *Marriage Boot Camp*. While on both series I kept my head in the game by reminding myself that business was always business.

The business of marriage naturally has its pitfalls, and I was prepared for the possibility of many of them. However, it never occurred to me that I would fall victim to one of the most overused rumors in entertainment: the closeted gay man. During an argument between Mimi and K. Michelle, K. Michelle mentioned that Johnny was gay and then casually threw out that we were roommates. Although she didn't directly come for me, the damage had been done. Regardless of the truth, the mere mention that Johnny was gay and I was his roommate insinuated enough for the rumors to fly. To the world, I was immediately a closeted gay man and the facts didn't matter. It bothered me that Johnny had been dragged into it all because he was still a college kid with a great heart and wet behind the ears. I couldn't stand by and not say anything. I felt protective over my friend and insulted by the blatant lies. In all of my years in the music business, no other artist had ever disrespected me like that. As much as it went against my normally calm demeanor, I had to react. That was like one of the only times that the audience saw me flip out on the show.

Even with the truth on my side and despite my protests, that one false comment led to me being questioned about everything. Any negative views that anyone had about me multiplied a million times over. It was that one bad seed is sown into a flourishing garden that soon strangled the life from the once beautiful flowers. When the public found out that Margeaux had an interest in women the questions really began to circulate. Everyone wanted to know if we were swingers and if we were both gay. There was no way to escape the rumors. My man Mark Twain said it best, "a lie can travel halfway around the world while the truth is putting on its shoes." If I am one thing, I am secure in my manhood, so I have nothing against gay men. In no way do I think being gay is a bad thing. However, being called gay when it's not true makes things harder for you in the music industry. I'm just glad that I have this book to clear things up. Maybe now people will hear me loud and clear.

AFTERWORD

My Scripted Reality

Today, being in the Mecca of everything Hollywood is great for me. Reality TV may have painted me a certain way, but I have to say it has opened a new door for me. Living out in LA made me see just how much talent is out there in the world and how people will do anything to make it. I guess since I was always the guy who hustled and made a way out of no way, I don't look at anything as "making it." Most of the talent that comes out in droves to LA won't make it, but I admire the drive. You have people linking up with people they don't know and getting a house together so that they can chase their dreams.

Then you have the people who come out here and get lost. I was in a club one night not too long ago, and I saw the most beautiful Asian girl I'd ever seen. I'm watching her and then all of a sudden, she bends over and snorts a line of coke. She was out in the open in front of everyone. She didn't even care that she was being watched. Why would a man from Brooklyn, New York be so shocked by something like that? I grew up seeing this all the time, but I realized that a lot of young people come to LA and get lost quickly. Some people are built for this life while others are trying to build this life, and there is a difference. That's why someone like Tyler Perry made it. To become homeless and end up sleeping in your car, you have to believe in what you want.

After all this, what did I learn? What would I have done differently? How can I move differently so that I don't end up dealing with the same things again, ten years from now? Am I really a changed man, not for the sake of proving something to the world, but for my personal growth? If you've made it to this point of my story, it's because you wanted the goods and you wanted the juice. I'm sure you weren't expecting a grown man to get this deep or to open up and allow God to do spiritual surgery in front of the world once again. I'm sitting here purging myself of the mess in my life that took place over the last four years and even before that. I'd be lying if I said all my problems started the moment I signed a contract with VH1.

I would be remiss not to acknowledge playing a large role in my destruction. Television just gave me a platform that showcased a fraction of my world. They fused two worlds together to create something you would enjoy - some true and some false. I wasn't sure how I wanted to close this out. What did I have left to say after I just poured blood, sweat, and tears into this book? Well, I think I owe it to all those women who played a major role in my life over the last five (ten for Margeaux) years. You may not like everything I have to say in this part, but I've been honest up to this point, and I won't stop now. They may never read, let alone acknowledge these words, but they are here for me. Here are the words I never said.

LETTERS

Dear Margeaux,

    I had every intention for us to live the dream we imagined for our relationship. I know we got married for the purpose of your green card and to build a future together, which is something I wanted more than anything. It may have been rushed, but there was a spark the moment I met you. You felt it, and so did I. How else could I have been able to agree to get married unless I felt it? On paper, it was rushed, but to me, it felt right. I realize now what we both lost with each other was the room to grow outside of each other. You had expressed feeling like you couldn't make certain moves without knowing who you were. I had expressed the need to make moves together, not once considering that you just need to grow into your own identity. We shared great moments together and lived like kids together. As a man, I admit I wasn't the best with my emotions and being attentive to your needs. Those needs allowed you to shut down on me and we ended up doing "business as usual" without considering the business of marriage. Just like when you draft a business plan and start to gather everything you'll need to build a sustainable business, we needed to do that with marriage. Maybe there was a part of me that thought you could teach me since you grew up seeing a functional, healthy marriage. Maybe there was a part of me that felt like where I was lacking; you might be able to pull me up. I'm man enough to admit that I didn't and still don't have all the answers. You cut off your emotions from me because of things I said and what I did

wasn't any better. Why is it that I thought I wasn't necessarily doing anything wrong just because we were flowing artistically? I feel like a lot of what I said, you misinterpreted my words and never really paid attention to my heart. I had good intentions, but intentions are just that. We got so far off balance until it was too late for the relationship. You fell for another man at your lowest point when your dad died, and I was so deaf to you calling out for the man you loved. The man you wanted to be right there with you going through your pain with you. I failed you, and I'm sorry. I missed one of the most important moments in your life. How could I be so numb and miss the cries and your calls for my affection, understanding, comfort and support? We were the real Bonnie & Clyde, the real ride or die type and no one can take that away from us. I will live the rest of my life remembering the good moments we had. We both grew into other people, or rather, we grew into who we were supposed to be, which eventually led to us seeing that we weren't right for each other. I'm just happy we can stay friends and that we had a chance to build some things that will remain around forever (great music). There will always be a place in my heart for you. I will never forget the times we shared and the bond we created.
I love you,
Nikko

Dear Mimi,

    We started out as two people who grew to know each other over the years. It was the entertainment life that helped us build a bridge to becoming close friends. We shared a great one night stand that lasted for years in memory, and every time I saw you throughout the years, we would greet each other with open arms and respect. I thank you for the opportunity for letting me be your co-star on the show. At a minimum, I'm thankful for that. The dark side got the best of both of us. Who knew it would be us once again together on a platform we didn't control and that took control of us? I don't blame you for anything. I blame myself for thinking you were strong enough to have my back against a network that had my character designed for me before I filmed my first scene with you on the show. I truly believe you're a good person; we just crossed paths again at a bad moment in both of our lives. I was in a broken marriage, and you were in a broken relationship. I believe if television wasn't in the way we could have had something great but when you enter into a world of the unknown anything and everything can happen. You had already been on the show before I came on, so I was hoping you would find a way to help me fall into the fabric of it all without us losing what we had. I guess that's my problem. How could I expect loyalty from you when you were still loyal to someone else? Even with all the heartache, he caused you; you still couldn't find the strength to see how our life could've been better, even when we weren't filming. I

thank you for at least considering me. You opened a door for me that gave me access. It gave me a look into a new world, even if that world ended up being cold. Now, I know how to play the game. I know how to take advantage of the opportunity without losing myself. I'm always able to see the great in something, even if it didn't feel great at the time. You took me out of my comfort zone by asking me to be on the show with you. I believe I was good to you, even if you don't want to admit it. I wish you and your family nothing but the best.
Love,
Nikko

Dear Mona,

I had been running into you for years around the music industry before *Love & Hip Hop* was even created. Who knew that when we connected again, it would be in television and not music? I watched you do your thing in music years before reality television was even widely accepted. I had a lot of respect for you back then. We used to speak to each other and acknowledge what we both brought to the music world. The television world was new for both of us, but I was wet behind the ears. We all have to do what we have to do to take care of ourselves and our families. But I feel there's a line you cross and a line you don't cross. Once you strip someone of their humanity, that's the line for me. I feel you had the control to at least give me some humanity and make me look halfway decent to the world. Instead, you chose to villainize me without mercy. You had a show to run, and I get it, but where is your human consciousness? I have a family to feed too, and the way I was displayed didn't leave any room for me to eat and make money for myself outside of the show. You took the worst part of my filming and made me out to be the devil with no human soul. That's not the Mona I met years ago. I'm not going to sit here and say that I knew you inside and out, but I never felt that I'd be sitting across from you and looking at you like we'd never encountered each other before.

Dear Monica,
We both caught each other at a vulnerable time in our lives. When I met you, we became cool through a mutual friend of ours. We hooked up three years later as a couple, with you hanging out with me and listening to my fucked up life on Love and Hip Hop. Ironically, that would draw us closer to one another. We started falling for each other; then we made our connection. We started building something. A life that I thought would last this time around. We used to talk on the phone every day while I was in Atlanta dealing with my exit on the show. You were my support system, and I was your rock. Moving in together once I got to Los Angeles was another turning point for me. I was over Atlanta at this point, and we

were starting something new. It felt good. I thought we were helping each other to grow in so many ways, but the pressure of having to find income put a strain on our relationship. We would have worked out if we never moved in together. We both saw sides of each other that made things ugly between us. I think you are a great woman with a big future ahead of you, but the timing was wrong for us. I have to say that I believe it was a blessing in disguise moving in together. Had we not, would I have been able to see the truth? Would I have been able to get to the root of the matter behind the drinking, the depression, and the fear? Would you have opened up to me without me seeing it up close and personal, day in and day out? Or perhaps, you felt like I mind as well be living alone. That's what you said so many times; you felt like I wasn't seeing or hearing you. Or maybe, just maybe, you were placed in my life as a mirror so that I could finally get to the root of my issues. I believe you can soar if you just get to the place where you figure out how to deal with life's dark days without losing your head. We all have some childhood scars to heal from, but don't let that stop you from being great, from moving into all that you've been called to be. I'm proud of you. I pray that you find the strength you need to make the changes necessary for your mental and emotional health.

Love always,
Nikko

Dear Dad,

    I am your clone in so many ways. You're like a big brother and a dad all in one. You gave me the light to keep going. When I understood the adversity and challenges you had gone through in your life; I got a better glimpse at the man. The fact that you didn't get the education you deserved and ended up dropping out of high school allowed me to understand where you may have felt limited, disadvantaged and unable to be the best you wanted to be. Regardless, I saw you become the true definition of a hustler and an investor in your own thoughts. It was like greatness manifested itself right before my very eyes. I looked up to you because of the love you have for humanity. You've always been a man of your word. Some may look at the fact that I didn't get to be with you all the time as bad parenting. I feel like when you said you would come and pick me up from my moms on weekends, you nailed it every time. I admit I wasn't the best son and didn't always listen to your guidance, but we still got along. You never made me feel like I couldn't make my own decisions or make me feel low when I didn't make a decision with which you agreed. If I had to describe a father, I would say it's a man who puts his family first in front of his wants and needs and goes the distance to provide by any means. One thing you taught me is that my siblings were important. You always made sure we had time together and that we could get to know one another, despite the fact that we lived in separate households. To this day, our bond is what it is

because of that. I'm glad we reunited again, after your years in prison. Being in Barbados with you allowed me to see how much you value spiritual growth and how much you intend to become better, no matter what you've done in the past. You can't blame a man for wanting to change, even if you don't understand how he's going about the change. I'm sure there were moments you saw me on television, and you shook your head. But to know that we can look at each other in the eyes, man to man and find a balance within our relationship to talk to one another, support one another and love each other unconditionally means a lot. Now we can walk into the future together and live another moment with more memories to tell. Thanks, Pop.
Love,
Nikko

———

Dear Mom,

You raised a rock, and you did it by any means necessary never making excuses of not having enough time or shelter to raise two boys. After hearing your story of your childhood how could I not grow up to be a king? I learned your childhood story when I was an adult and ever since that day the light of your strength guided me through the dark side of the street life. You still found the willpower to take care of two of your siblings while the three of you were homeless. To make matters more difficult, you never had a mother around to nurture you or show you how to be a woman. Your father wasn't always there, but you figured it all out. That to me is a leader. You represent everything a rebel, survivor, hero, mother, grandmother and inspiration to all women of race and color. You never judged or turned your back on me. You've always encouraged, pushed, believed, excepted, loved and prayed for my brother and me to be the best we could, in spite of how bad things were. You always supplied what you could but made sure we were always presentable at home and in public for any occasion. If there were a mother award of the year, you would win every year for being consistent with your love.

You always accepted most of my decisions, knowing that my decision would shape me into the man you saw as a boy. Even when I wasn't humanized on television and they devalued my character to being a person without a heart and a womanizer without a soul, you still told me to keep going. You would encourage me that my time is coming! You taught me how to weather the storm and stand for who I am, and I did. I want to say I love you as my mother, friend and as my rock. No matter how many females come and go, you will always have the number one spot in my heart.
I love you endlessly,
Nikko

Nikko London is a reality TV personality, music producer, songwriter and fitness enthusiast who was born and raised in Brooklyn, New York. The world was introduced to Nikko as he appeared on the second season of VH1's hit reality show, *Love & Hip Hop: Atlanta*. Although reality television brought him into millions of homes Nikko's God-given musical talents will eventually make him a household name.

Music has always been a refuge for Nikko, as a child he would escape through a great piece of music, creating his own wonderland! At the tender age of 10 he began rapping as a past time in the streets of Brooklyn; soon after he discovered his unique ear for music.

As Nikko set out to build a career in the entertainment industry, he wanted to set himself apart from other hopefuls. In doing so, he studied several genres of music such as reggae, soul, rock and roll, and gospel. Nikko has worked with award winning producers such as Timbaland and Sean Garret. He's also worked with songstress Tamia, and hip hop heavyweight Rick Ross just to name a few. In 2012, Nikko upped the ante cementing his dedication to music by forming his own production company, "Unstoppable Records." Currently, Nikko is working on his own projects.

CPSIA information can be obtained
at www.ICGtesting.com
Printed in the USA
LVOW12s2048170417
531113LV00001B/1/P